The Education of

Black People

Ten Critiques 1906-1960

by W.E.B. Du Bois

Edited by Herbert Aptheker

Monthly Review Press • *New York*

Contents

vii   Introduction

PART I

3   Preface
5   The Hampton Idea (1906)
17   Galileo Galilei (1908)
31   The College-bred Community (1910)
41   Diuturni Silenti (1924)
61   Education and Work (1930)
83   The Field and Function of the Negro College (1933)
103   The Revelation of Saint Orgne the Damned (1938)

PART II

127   Editor's Note
129   The Future of the Negro State University (1941)
139   The Future and Function of the Private
       Negro College (1946)
149   Whither Now and Why (1960)

159   Bibliography of the Published Writings of
       W. E. B. Du Bois on Education

169   Index

Introduction

While William Edward Burghardt Du Bois's published works reached almost incredible proportions, in his Papers he left a vast collection of *unpublished* sketches, essays, journals, and even several books. In the body of his work, the present book is unique for it consists of both published and unpublished writings by the late Dr. Du Bois; it is, however, in largest part a book that he himself planned. Indeed, it was very nearly published early in the 1940s; since that is the book's beginnings, it might be well for its Introduction also to commence at that point.

In late February or very early March, 1940, Du Bois—then chairman of the Sociology Department at Atlanta University in Georgia—submitted the manuscript of a book, which he entitled "Seven Critiques of Negro Education, 1908–1938," to the University of North Carolina Press in Chapel Hill. On March 6, 1940, Mary T. Bobbit, secretary to William T. Couch, then the Press Director, acknowledged, with thanks, receipt of the manuscript and promised: "As soon as possible, we will give our attention to this work and let you know our decision in regard to it." [1]

That same month the manuscript commenced its round of Press readers. Among these was Edgar W. Knight (1886–1953), Professor of Education at the university and at that time also chairman of the Commission on Curricula Problems and Research of the Southern Association of Colleges and Secondary Schools. In May the manuscript was read by Howard W. Odum (1884–1954), Professor of Sociology at the university. Profes-

---

1. Letter in the Du Bois Papers, in custody of the editor. The original title of the book was as given above, including the error in date, since the first essay was dated 1906. The error is somewhat characteristic of Du Bois who was very careful about almost everything except dates; in any case his artistic soul would prefer the symmetry of 1908–1938.

sor Odum, who had been President of the American Sociology Society in 1930, was in 1940 director of the Institute for Research in Social Science of the University of North Carolina. On May 24, 1940, the manuscript was passed on to Henry M. Wagstaff (1876–1945) who had been for over thirty years Professor of History at the university. Mr. Wagstaff returned the manuscript a month later. It may be presumed that the Director of the Press, himself a well-known author, [2] also examined the manuscript with care.

All seemed to have been favorably impressed, for Mr. Couch, in a letter to Du Bois dated September 21, 1940, stated that the Press's Board of Governors had authorized publication, if the finance committee gave final approval. Couch thought the latter committee would give its approval but doubted that the book would do more than "pay for itself." He suggested, therefore, that if and when a contract were forthcoming it probably would provide for no royalty payment until after the first thousand copies had been sold and that then a payment of ten percent of the retail price—which would not exceed $2—would be offered. Couch added that the "European situation"—meaning the Second World War which had just commenced—might upset any plans for the future.

Three days later Du Bois responded, acknowledging the letter and writing:

> I am quite willing to have you publish my book on the financial basis which you mention. I have never received much income from my books but on the other hand I do not think that any publisher has actually lost money. In any case the money consideration is the least thing I have in mind in writing. [3]

2. Mr. Couch in 1945 moved on to become Director of the Press at the University of Chicago and more recently has been chief editor of several leading encyclopedias issuing from New York City. A copy of the manuscript record (No. 1166) was kindly sent to the editor on June 22, 1972, by Mrs. Jeanne C. Smith, assistant to the current Press Director; she informed the editor that no further documents on this manuscript were available.

3. The Couch—Du Bois letters are in the Du Bois Papers.

On the history of this manuscript, nothing else seems to have survived, except for a note on the "manuscript record" of the University of North Carolina Press which reads "Ret'd to author 2–19–41. Press unable to publish at present for financial reasons."

No evidence survives in the Du Bois Papers that he thereafter made any attempt to publish this volume;[4] when he left New York for Ghana, however, in 1961, while he deposited many of his books and some of his Papers in the library at Fisk University and placed in the custody of the present editor all of his correspondence and the bulk of his unpublished writings, this manuscript he took with him. The editor came upon it in May, 1971, when he and his wife were the guests of Mrs. Du Bois in Cairo and were working on the additional Papers in her possession.

The book now in the reader's hands consists of the seven essays selected by Du Bois for the 1940 volume and three additional ones, dated 1941, 1946, and 1960, selected by the editor. Each of the original seven is introduced by a brief note written by Du Bois and is followed by equally brief comment upon the address's reception, also written by him; this material is published here for the first time and was written by Du Bois for the projected Chapel Hill volume. In addition, the second essay, "Galileo Galilei," delivered in 1908, has hitherto not been published and appears in print now for the first time.

Du Bois edited these addresses for the book he had in mind; the manuscript has been compared line by line with the published versions and changes of any consequence at all are noted at the appropriate places. The manuscript as a whole has been published as written by Du Bois, of course; the editor has added an occasional footnote and corrected factual slips and typographical errors. Du Bois did not provide the place of publication of the six essays previously published in his manuscript; this information will be found in the bibliography of his writings on education which the editor has compiled and appended to this volume.

4. With the exception of a letter to publishers Reynal and Hitchcock in 1943: see p. 127.

The three essays selected for inclusion by the editor, and forming Part II of this volume, complete the presentation of Du Bois's views on education and represent, it is believed, the fullest expression of those views as they developed in the last quarter century of his life.

It will not be inappropriate, perhaps, for the editor to comment upon the substance of the essays that follow. In the lifetime of their author, no one in the United States was more expert in the area of the nature, theory, and purposes of education; and on the specific subject of the education of Black people in the United States, Du Bois had no peer.

In the analysis which he offers of education, emphases and aspects change, naturally, for Du Bois was never rigid and advocated and practiced both criticism and self-criticism; further, of course, the time-range of these essays covers over fifty years—and fifty years which witnessed greater changes in the life of humanity probably than any preceding half century in history. But there are certain constants and these deserve emphasis in terms both of their own consequence and also in terms of comprehending W. E. B. Du Bois.

The reader will find a persistent demand—explicit or assumed—for excellence in education and this especially in fundamental skills: reading, writing, counting and, above all, thinking. He will find the demand for sacrifice, for a life of service, and an insistence that while such a life will bring hardships and temptations it also will bring fulfillment; an insistence that, in any case, only with such a life has one *lived*. In this affirmation, there runs also Du Bois's particular feeling about his own people; that their own history has forced into their bones and hearts the ideas of service, of compassion, of justice.

In emphasizing excellence, Du Bois calls particularly for the mastery of the humanities and the sciences, with special attention to economics and mathematics. He views education as a life-long process; and while his words stress its seriousness, there also was in Du Bois what he called "The Joy of Living." He was a wonderfully *happy* man and he wanted those for whom he spoke and wrote to get that sense of joy in battle, joy in trying, and joy in accomplishing.

Du Bois saw education as a process of the teaching of certain central values: moderation, an avoidance of luxury, a concern for courtesy, a capacity to endure, a nurturing of love for beauty. He saw education as basic to the production of what—in his youth—people called *character*.

Du Bois saw education (to be truly education) as partisan and—given the realities of the social order—fundamentally subversive. Specifically, in this connection, he wrote as a Black man in the United States; in this sense he was concerned in the first place with the education of his people in the United States, and that education as part of the process of the liberation of his people. Thus, his writing on education—as on everything else—has a kind of national consciousness, a specific motivation which—while directed towards his people—at the same time and therefore was meant to serve all humanity. Thus, he conveys a sense of pride in his people, but this is never false and is accompanied by sharp criticism where he feels the latter to be justified; but the pride and love above all shine through his writing. He also had a sense of urgency for he knew, in his own flesh, how awful was the crucifixion and how vital was the sense of progress. He insistently calls for great energy and initiative; for Black people controlling their own lives and for continued experimentation and innovation.

Withal, there always is present in Du Bois the devotion to fact, the need to face reality and the fierce—almost fanatical—insistence upon integrity. Finally, the essays that follow should convey the sheer courage of Du Bois: let the reader consider the circumstances, for instance, under which he gave his speeches of 1906, 1908, 1924—all three in the South, and the pre-New Deal South at that.

Du Bois's writing reflected the male-supremacist bias of our language and he repeatedly writes of men or boys when in fact he means men and women and boys and girls. This was, however, purely verbal with Du Bois; for, in fact, he was eras ahead of his time on the question of the rights and capacities and position of women as he was on most other significant social questions. In the case of Du Bois one has evidence of this going back to an editorial he wrote for the *Fisk Herald* in December 1887, where he hailed the fact, as it seemed to him, that "The age of Woman is surely dawning." He was an early and persistent and militant advocate of full political and economic rights for women. This is not the place to develop this aspect of Du Bois but since in the essays that follow his use of male terms when he means human beings is so common, one should note that he made his generic usage of "men" quite explicit very early in his writing career. Thus, in an essay entitled "The Negro Ideals of Life" (published in *The Christian Register,* Boston, October 26, 1905), one finds:

> Who are Men? . . . It is not simply the capitalists who
> are men . . . it is not simply the laborers, it is not simply
> the men who are men, but men's mothers and daughters,
> too, and finally the world of men holds men of many
> colors and races, and it is not white men alone who aspire
> to life's higher ideals, and demand the possibility of their
> realization.

The editor expresses, again, his profound appreciation for the participation in producing this volume—as of everything else he has ever tried to do—of his wife, Fay P. Aptheker. His gratitude to Mrs. Du Bois for her encouragement and her confidence cannot be expressed adequately with words.

September, 1972   HERBERT APTHEKER

The Education of

Black People

Preface

Seven times in seventy years—mostly in the last thirty —it has seemed my duty to criticize and evaluate the education of American Negroes.[1] Mostly, but not wholly, I have talked of college training at critical times in the career of various well-known Negro colleges, because I regard the college as the true founding stone of all education, and not as some would have it, the kindergarten. These speeches were made at various times at well-known institutions: one each was made at Hampton and Howard, four at Fisk, and one to a New England audience. Of the speeches at Fisk only two applied specifically to Fisk; the other two were of general application, and I made those because as an alumnus I made my Alma Mater my forum. The speeches represent in each case my firm conviction and emotional reaction against certain trends and facts which I wished to oppose or forward. The spoken word is not usually an attractive form of literature shorn as it must be of its responsive living audience. As I looked these talks over, my first temptation was to edit them into a statement of my present views. But on reflection, it seemed to me better if they were left standing as they are, as a sort of living record of reaction, written out before delivery and set down with some care. They would in a way tell more of what Negroes have been thinking concerning the development of their education especially in the colleges. I am, therefore, publishing these seven talks with explanations of their occasion and some of the results of their delivery.

Atlanta, 1940   W. E. B. DU BOIS

1. Du Bois means here that he had reached his seventieth year in 1938; in the original manuscript, of course, his speeches spanned a period of thirty-two years.

The Hampton Idea

*In 1906 the United States was obsessed with what may be
called the Hampton-Tuskegee idea of Negro education.
It was in a sense logical and sincere and I would have
said in 1900 that I believed in it, but not as a complete
program. I believed that we should seek to educate a
mass of ignorant sons of slaves in the three R's and the
technique of work in a sense of the necessity and duty
of good work. But beyond this, I also believed that such
schools must have teachers, and such a race must have
thinkers and leaders, and for the education of these folk
we needed good and thorough Negro colleges.*

*For several years I attended the Negro conferences
held in the summer at Hampton, with the idea of knitting
together in thought and statement the case of higher
education and industrial education. But it was in vain.
The resolutions passed by these conferences mentioned
everything except the Negro college; for instance, in 1902
under "education," agriculture, manual training, religious
training, normal schools, and kindergartens were
mentioned. There was mention of business, religion,
domestic economy, and sanitation, but not a word was
said about the Negro college. This continued for several
years. I did not obtrude my views. After all, I was a
guest and after publication of my criticism of Booker T.
Washington in the* Souls of Black Folk, *in 1903, I was
under a certain suspicion. But I said to myself, "I am
going to stop attending these conferences until I am
especially asked to speak, and then I am going to say
precisely what I think." The invitation came in the
summer of 1906. It was with something of that
inexplicable but magnificent confidence of youth that I
stood before a smug Hampton and spoke.*

5

I have chosen a theme tonight which seems to me most weighty and important—that contains in a way the kernel of that message which I have been called to give to men.[1] I am to speak of Self-Assertion and the Higher Education: I am going to point out the Great Lack which faces our race in the modern world, Lack of Energy; and the Great Fear that consciously and unconsciously grips the world lest that Lack be supplied. I want to say that this will be partially realized in the inevitable and needful assertion of the self in each of us—the self of the race, the self of the individual—the soul of the man and soul of the man's world. Further than this I particularly wish to impress upon you that this forceful, often rude, but always mighty, assertion of the human self needs a curbing and a balancing—a niceness of concentering and adjustment—in fine an education, and an education which is higher and more important and more infinitely meaningful for the world and its wide ideals, than any of the other kinds of important but subordinate training which men must have. And finally, I will say that this strongly asserted but balanced self—this fully self-conscious but cultured soul—will move toward a perfectly definite and clearly conceived goal without faltering or hesitation and from that goal to goals beyond and so forever onward.

1. As originally published, this address begins with the following paragraph:"I have been asked to come to Hampton to talk to teachers and therefore it is especially to the teachers of the summer school that this paper is addressed; the other listeners who have so kindly come must bear with us while we commune together. I speak all the more gladly to you young teachers for two great reasons: first and selfishly, because I am a teacher, and therefore, the problems that front you are peculiarly my problems, and the toil of my life is your toil; but secondly and chiefly, because you are the type and representative of that fateful class through whom the great army of tomorrow's men are learning the riddle of the world, the meaning of life and the life worth living. And so when I speak to you, I feel that in a peculiar way I am speaking to the future world and that if I say well what I am moved to say and force my words into your souls then somehow and sometime those words will fire the hearts of men.

And therefore [continuing as above]."

This is my theme tonight, and for whatever heresy it contains in time and place I beg your indulgence. For in the world this alone is necessary—that if a man speak and act, he speak and act the truth and not a lie. [2]

What is it that in the modern world this race of ours most clearly lacks—what is our greatest need, our greatest failing? At first thought I suppose few persons would agree in the answer to this question: one would say education, one would say wealth, some would think patience and some would think it was ability, especially organizing ability. And yet most of these answers would be comprehended in the one answer which I shall give: Energy. The great Lack of the Negro race and of nearly all the darker races today is Energy, self-assertiveness, the command and use of at least its more conspicuous powers.

Nor is this racial indolence or ease of life a fault or badge of inferior gift or development. It simply represents a defense of tropical races against a tropical sun. No hurried, worried race could ever have risen out of the blazing suns of Africa—rather conditions of living there demand that languid dalliance with nature and her wants which we crudely and harshly call the laziness of the tropics. And this indolence has come down to us by heredity—not that uncertain and doubtful physical heredity of which we talk far more than we know, but by that immensely more important cause of human rhythmic action which we call social heredity, and social heredity is another way of saying that in general we act and think as our neighbors do and that our closest neighbors are our parents and grandparents. Nor does the lack of energy which we as a race bring down in unconscious imitation of our fathers deserve today to be denominated laziness. We are not lazy; we work, we work continuously; and more of us work than do other Americans; rather this racial trait of ours today shows itself in a certain lack of initiative—a timidity in doing: a want of self-confidence, self-assertiveness, and self-knowledge—a kind of spiritual hesitation in a world where spirit rules.

2. In the original this sentence follows: "Let me then begin with the Great Lack."

Now the world knows this and the American world above all frequently points to it, and yet when the manifest antidote appears, when the remedy is pointed out, when the course of procedure, which will turn indolence into energy, hesitation into confidence, and diffidence into self-assertion—when the well-known and world-tried methods of human awakening are mentioned in regard to us and ours, there falls a strange and ominous hush on the voices of the world; and spoken or unspoken, there arises the Great Fear.

Now the Great Fear has been variously named and designated—it has been called in the past, Mob-Rule, Sans-Cullotism, the Yellow Peril, the Negro Problem, and Social Equality. Whatever it is called, the foundation of the Great Fear is this: when a human being becomes suddenly conscious of the tremendous powers lying latent within him, when from the puzzled contemplation of a half-known self, he rises to the powerful assertion of a self, conscious of its might, then there is loosed upon the world possibilities of good or of evil that make men pause. And when this happens in the case of a class or nation or a race, the world fears or rejoices according to the way in which it has been trained to contemplate a change in the conditions of the class or race in question. . . . [3]

And thus today the Great Fear is speaking among men. It is voicing itself more or less articulately against all the darker

3. The ellipses are in the original manuscript as prepared by Du Bois. The omission constitutes a paragraph, as follows: "In the sixteenth century the peasants of Germany heard a voice. They realized their degradation and the sweat of the wrongs stank upon them. With the voice of Martin Luther came sudden consciousness of their power. They rose in mad fury, fought and pillaged, burned and murdered, until Luther aghast raised his rough voice in anathema against them and the leagued nobility beat them like whipped dogs back to their serfdom again. Why? Were the peasants wrong? No, they were cruelly oppressed and shamelessly mistreated. But, argued the good men of that day, oppression is better than anarchy—beware how you raise in the hearts of the lower classes ambitions that can never be fulfilled— self-assertion that courts annihilation. Thus the Great Fear showed itself in the sixteenth century."

races, but more particularly against those of Negro descent. It says in its saner moments: these Negroes—they are, humanly-speaking, brothers; they have some rights and deserve some opportunities; but deal carefully with them. Put their rights in the background; emphasize their duties—say little of ambition or aspiration; and above all, watch and ward against the first appearance of arrogance or self-assertion or consciousness of great power. Take the eyes of these millions off the stars and fasten them in the soil; and if their young men will dream dreams, let them be dreams of corn bread and molasses.

There has thus arisen what may be called the soothing syrup attitude toward the race problem. This consists in the frequent administration of sweet and pleasant doses so compounded as to put the unwary to sleep and stop his incessant complaints.

This then, young men and women, is the situation: the necessary indolence of our fathers is unsuited to a more active age and more rigorous climate. Yet the world has always feared itself and particularly feared the unconscious substratum. "When the sleeper wakes," it has ever cried, "Beware!" Consequently, there has risen up a policy of harsh repression and gentle discouragement toward you and me and the children we teach, lest in our awakening from our racial indolence to the feverish activity and self-assertion of this modern age we bring catastrophe upon the nation.

Under such circumstances, what is our duty, particularly our duty toward those children whom we are educating? For education is by derivation and in fact a drawing out of human powers. If the extent and character of this development is itself a matter of world dispute, how shall we govern ourselves?

First we must carefully understand the age in which we live; above all, we must realize that this is an age of tremendous activity; that today no race which is not prepared to put forth the full might of its carefully developed powers can hope to maintain itself as a world power. On one point, therefore, there can be no question—no hesitation: unless we develop our full capabilities, we cannot survive. If we are to be trained grudgingly and suspiciously; trained not with reference to what we can be, but with sole reference to what somebody wants us to be; if instead of following the methods pointed out by the accumulated wisdom of the world for the development of full human power, we simply are trying to follow the line of least resistance and teach black men only such things and by such methods as are momentarily popular, then my fellow teachers, we are going to fail and fail ignominiously in our attempt to raise the black race to its full humanity and with that failure falls the fairest and fullest dream of a great united humanity.

If then beyond peradventure or doubt we must strive to develop this Negro race to its very utmost, making them men and not half men, then there comes the great question How? Here the experience of the world comes to our aid: mere self-assertion—the crude putting forth of powers of which the boy or man has suddenly become conscious, does not in any case mean the fullness of a man's powers; to this initial energy must succeed the long and careful process of coordination and development, the balancing and repression, the inspiration and encouragement. The fullness of this process is a matter of a man's whole life, but the beginning of it and the most important part of it— the crucial and critical period of its effective fulfillment, is in the years which we call specifically and peculiarly the years of education. And we call the higher education that part of human training which is devoted specifically and peculiarly into bringing the man into the fullest and roundest development of his powers as a human being.

While most persons of all ages would without hesitation admit this definition, yet the peculiar character of each age has stamped and changed the practical application of this higher training. . . .[4] Today in European culture we have just passed a peculiar and striking period of history. Always in all ages there went on coordinate with the higher training in human development, a training in the technical methods of earning a living. For life with all its higher ends and aims must be a grim struggle with starvation and exposure. In earlier days the training by which men got food and clothes and shelter was not given in schools. The slaves and serfs who attended to this work were not supposed to be subjects for education at all. In the nineteenth century of our era, however, there came a tremendous mechanical development. So that never before have so many of the physical wants of the world been so well satisfied with so small an expenditure of human energy. On the other hand, development in the higher things of life has naturally fallen behind in this advance—our system of justice, our political life, our moral standards can scarcely be said to have advanced permanently and perceptibly for 2,000 years.

Naturally now with this tremendous emphasis on the technique of earning a living and with the enormous success in this struggle with the jealous material world, there has come a reflex influence on human education. The first evidence of this is the raising of technical education out of the homes and above haphazard methods, into great schools and into careful methods of training. But the influence has not stopped here. On the contrary, there has come a distinct philosophy of education which makes the earning of a living the center and norm of human training and which moreover dogmatically asserts that the subject matter and methods of work peculiar to technical schools are the best for all education—that outside them there is properly no higher training. Longer training a man may have, but no higher—the highest and best training is that which enables a man to earn a living.

Now it is this particular philosophy of education from which I have come here frankly to dissent and to express my dissent to you as teachers as strongly as I am able. And I do this the more willingly, because Hampton is the center of this, as I regard it, educational heresy, and because with all the striking history of this school, the noble lives given to its upbuilding, and the peculiar efficiency of its present organization, there is always present a tone which, as it seems to me, contradicts and

4. The ellipses are in the original manuscript; omitted was: "In Greece for instance the higher training became very largely aesthetics and literature suited to a nation of artists and philosophers, but leaving fatal gaps in the fuller human training. So too Rome trained her jurists and administrators in a way never since surpassed, but again failed in her larger and broader outlook."

almost sneers at the wonderful ideals which founded this great school.

Of course I know that this characterization of the Hampton philosophy is largely a matter of personal interpretation, and yet, in an institution where the President of the United States can with applause tell young men not to hitch their wagons to a star, but to a mule; where the sincere old man who spoke on this platform three days ago, can say amid laughter that the great duty of a minister is to teach his flock to raise a good dinner; and where around all and in all, there is an insistence on the practical in a manner and tone that would make Socrates an idiot and Jesus Christ a crank—in such a place it seems to me no infringement of the rights of hospitality to say that I believe that this doctrine is so fundamentally false as to call for a word of warning.[5]

I know that all these incidents I have mentioned are capable of an interpretation which has its measure of truth. I know that the great duty before you and me and our people today is to earn a living; and yet—and yet, there is in these doctrines an ineradicable falsification of truth and human history, and I am alarmed not so much that you are going to be misled by the untruth lurking in the truth, as I am alarmed at the case of the students you teach. No one can go through Hampton and believe that the world is simply bread and butter—they know that it is earth and air—the wonderful, gleaming sea, and the ver-

5. President Theodore Roosevelt delivered an extemporaneous address to the students and faculty of Hampton Institute on May 30, 1906. He spoke at Hampton after having spoken earlier the same day at a review of Confederate and Union veterans at Portsmouth, Virginia; upon the latter occasion he praised "both sides" equally for "fidelity to a high ideal. . . ." At Hampton he insisted that vocational work was the best for the "average" person of all colors; to his immediate audience he urged them to "take up agricultural work." The Hampton remarks are in the *Atlanta Constitution*, May 31, 1906; the address at Portsmouth is in the *New York Times*, May 31, 1906.

The morning session, June 28, 1906, of the Hampton Conference was devoted to a discussion of the work of Black ministers; it was

dure of flower and fruit. But when you as teachers, have learned a certain Hampton[6] way of expressing yourselves, I am wondering and anxiously wondering, just what picture of the world and life your students are getting.

Now I have said that in order to match the great demands of this age we need to throw off our indolence and use and develop every power that God has given us, and that the higher education is a method of developing these powers. Does this mean that college-bred men, trained in the technique of industry, receive as a matter of fact nothing broader than this![7] By no means. There is a sort of false distinction in these matters that has grown up and which does mischief. The college training is supposed to be chiefly ornamental and partly useless; interesting to such as have time, money, and inclination but otherwise not to be indulged in. On the other hand, industrial training is accused of confining itself to purely technical work after a fashion which is simply untrue of any industrial school.

As a matter of fact the college curriculum or the curriculum of the industrial school depends not so much on its content—on its actual studies, as on its aim. The aim of the higher training of the college is the development of power, the training of a self whose balanced assertion will mean as much as possible for the great ends of civilization. The aim of technical training on the

---

chaired by a Rev. E. O. P. Cheak of Farmville, Va. His opening remarks were in agreement with the content of Du Bois's description but were not literally affirmed—at least as given in the printed proceedings. Others, however, spoke at that session but their remarks were not printed. Since Du Bois spoke soon thereafter to an audience that—like himself—was present, presumably he was quoting accurately, if not precisely, remarks made at the conference. (Hampton Institute Press in 1906 published the *Tenth Annual Report of the Hampton Negro Conference.*)

6. The word "Hampton" does not occur in the original.

7. In the original, this sentence reads as follows: "Does this mean that college-bred men should not be trained to earn a living or that men trained in the technique of industry receive as a matter of fact nothing broader than this!"

other hand is to enable the student to master the present methods of earning a living in some particular way. Incidentally the college may and often does give some technical training; incidentally and always the industrial school teaches more than mere technique. It is no criticism of the college to say that its graduates are not technically efficient, just as the industrial school cannot justly be criticized for not turning out men of culture.

But the attitude that we as Negroes must take toward these two kinds of training is this: just as far as the race can afford it we must give to our youth a training designed above all to make them men of power, of thought, of trained and cultivated taste; men who know whither civilization is tending and what it means. The ideal would be to train every man in this way, and toward this ideal we tend. But today only a few can have such training because the time and labor of most men is needed for providing for the world's physical wants. Consequently we must select the most promising [for this broader, higher education];[8] and I sincerely hope that you will ever be alert to select from your students those of talent and promise and impress them with the fact that life is more than living—that necessary as it is to earn a living, it is more necessary and important to earn a life: that is to do for the world—its thought, its aspiration, its human value—so much that the world will not always continue to ask if life is worth living.

Impress it upon your pupils that potatoes and cows are only valuable because of the heaped up sacrifice, the midnight musing, the morning dreams of men who did not have potatoes enough to keep them alive. Send these talented boys to college—urge them and push them through, remembering that never in God's world is this Negro race going to hold its place in the world, until it shows by its fully developed and carefully trained powers its undoubted ability to do so. This is true. Men know it is true and I am particularly sorry that the college-bred men who write the Hampton conference resolutions have never found courage to say in this matter what they really believe.

8. Words bracketed by the editor do not appear in the original.

After we have sent our most promising to college, then not only the rest, but the college men too, need training in technical schools for the actual technique. Hampton Institute, instead of giving the world the impression that she has no use for college training, ought systematically to attract colored college graduates to post-graduate courses in technique; indeed just as the colleges need technique to complete their training of men for actual life, so the sad and crying need for industrial schools is men with culture and training enough in the broader humanities really to profit by the great technical opportunities of a plant like this.

When now we have gained for our race training in modern industry, and for our national leaders, self-assertion through a higher training in life and thought and power, then we can move toward the goal. What is that goal? It is at present one great Ideal: the abolition of the color line; the treatment of all men according to their individual desert and not according to their race. This is the one straight way of the Lord, despite all the devious paths which our friends and enemies suggest. Toward this I am pointing you tonight, my young friends. Toward this the voice of Ages points—a voice crying in the wilderness: "Make straight the way of the Lord."

ENVOY

This was said in 1906 and it was not until 1936 that I was invited back to Hampton. The Hampton folk of 1906 were outraged at my words. Many considered that I had abused their hospitality. But I thought at the time that I was speaking the truth, and as I read the speech over today there is not much that I would change. When I went back to Hampton in 1936, behold, Hampton had become a college and was wondering what to do with her industrial equipment! Indeed so complete was the transformation, that in after years I again took Hampton to task for surrendering the Hampton idea so entirely.

Galileo Galilei

1908

*It was in a spirit of stern and lofty criticism that I spoke
at Fisk University in 1908, twenty years after my
graduation. Much had happened in those years and even
in the two years since I had spoken at Hampton. Erastus
Cravath, the fine and stately first president of Fisk, died
in 1901. In accordance with missionary custom a retired
minister was put in his place. It was an unfair task to put
upon James G. Merrill. He was a kindly man sixty-eight
years of age and did not recognize the change taking
place in Negro education. The old afflatus of
Reconstruction times and the crusading teacher had gone,
and the problem of supporting education by passing the
hat was beginning to appear. He was not equal to the
task; few people were. Indeed in the end the whole
scheme broke down. But Dr. Merrill thought he saw a
ray of light. My college schoolmate, Maggie Murray,
became the second wife of Booker T. Washington in
1893. Dr. Merrill thought that through Washington's
influence some help might come from monied interests
to Fisk University; and to lure this philanthropy he
proposed to make certain changes in the Fisk curriculum.*

*Abruptly in the catalogue of 1906–07, Fisk advertised
a new department of "Applied Science." This was to be
accomplished by a modification and enlargement of old
courses and by the introduction of new ones aggregating
over 2,500 hours of instruction additional per year. The
money was furnished by the General Education Board,
the citizens of Nashville, the Slater Fund, and others.
There was added to the faculty an associate professor of
agriculture and associate professor of mechanical arts.
The college work in this department consisted of five
courses in agriculture, including animal husbandry,*

plant breeding, structural botany, and rural engineering. In the mechanical arts, came practical courses in architectural drawing, woodwork, and the theory of machines. In domestic science and art, came cooking and sewing. In 1907 and 1908 the teachers of agriculture and mechanical arts became full professors. Two women directed cooking and sewing in both these years.

On the face of it, the proposed department did not look genuine. First of all it was going to teach agriculture without a farm and on the limestone rocks of the city of Nashville. In the second place only two teachers were detailed for all this work, and they were teaching not simply college students but high school and even elementary students. There was no machinery or adequate laboratory. Two other persons who had long been teaching cooking and sewing in the high school and normal courses were regarded as parts of this new department. There was no way in which this proposed department could be regarded as the beginning of a technical or engineering school of college rank. At best it was a poor imitation of what Hampton and Tuskegee were struggling to do.

All this seemed to many of the alumni and to me as a Surrender and a Lie: the surrender of college training to the current industrial fad, without the honest effort and equipment which this entailed. We were alarmed. We were fighting for academic life. We were striving for the survival of the Negro college in a day of starvation and ridicule. A current anecdote going the rounds was true enough to be false: one dark collegian asks another: "Is you done yo' Greek?" I remember that George E. Haynes, a graduate of Fisk, then a student in the New York School of Social Work and afterward founder of the Urban League, came to me hot-foot in Atlanta. He said, "You are sure to be invited to speak on your twentieth reunion. You must help save Fisk. She is surrendering to industrialism." I was excited and my crusading spirit aroused. Perhaps we were over-fearful, *but I thought then that I was stemming a tide, and so I spoke to the graduating class.*

The man whom we know as Galileo was born in 1564 and died in 1642: born just after Elizabeth of England ascended the throne and died as the Thirty Years' War was about to end; and yet this tells us little until we understand the meaning of the age in which he lived—the waning sixteenth and the dawning seventeenth centuries; and unless above all it happens that we catch tonight the peculiar way in which his life and problems concern us and our problems both as individuals and as graduates of Fisk University.

Galileo was born of noble rank in Pisa which we all know for its leaning tower and bronze doors, but which stood then for a memory and a prophecy—a memory of former glory of artist, merchant, and warrior, there where its marble palaces cunning in handiwork looked down on the river Arno and the sea.

He became a learner and teacher of men and in this life career what did he accomplish three hundred years ago? The simple unexplained record is in itself wonderful: he found the law of falling bodies; he invented the telescope; he discovered the moons of Jupiter, he explained the reflected light of planets; he laid down the laws of cohesion; he studied the law of the pendulum and applied it to the clock; and above all he adduced irrefragable proof of the correctness of the Copernican doctrine that the sun and not the earth is the center of our universe. Simply and barely stated this accomplishment is tremendous. To few human beings has it been given, in a life of four-score years, to advance so momentously the sum of human knowledge.

But this bare recounting does not do justice to his genius. Judge this World Genius not simply by the things he learned, but rather by the ignorance of his Age. This was a day when falling and gravitation were things too slight for human minds to ponder over; when the sky was regarded as a decorated changeable roof of the world; when time depended on sundials and hourglasses; and when the grand old legend of Joshua and the sun in Ajalon was regarded as a plain and literal statement of fact. It was a day when men assumed knowledge of the whole Truth and argued down to the individual fact, instead of ceaselessly, endlessly, and minutely studying the fact and then guessing as we do today cautiously at the mighty shadow of Reality. Here then was a human soul that walked into this world naked and unashamed, that dared to see what his own eyes saw and think whither his own clear logic went. A dangerous soul—a Revolutionist greater than Robespierre, a socialist wilder than Marx or Gorky—a very creator of a new heaven and a new earth.

And here if I were minded I might end, with this triumphant record, and with a dim hint at jealousy o'erpassed and persecution surmounted, of physical blindness and suffering ignored, celebrate a triumphant death in the year of Newton's birth; and tell of the tomb that sits today in Florence to his honor—there where the golden Arno fragrant with memories sings to the sea beneath the olive-crowned marbles of Lorenzo the Magnificent.

But it is in such half-finished biography that men do mischief in the world and blind the eyes of young men and women like these graduates here. It sweeps dust in their eyes and discord in their ears, and to the eternal thunder of the questioning, "How?" it returns only the answer to the answerd question, "What?" Easy it is to tell what men have done in this world—Lincoln freed the slave, Grant freed Lincoln, and Hamilton made us a nation. But how—How? ask the men who will do. Stars there are; them we see and know, but—How do men reach them?—What of the Way, the Power, and the Opposition?

So in Galileo's life I want to turn to three things: what was the Impulse that gave him power to do? What were the Obstacles he encountered? And How did he surmount them?

The impulse was a new vision of the world. From the time of Dante in the thirteenth up to the blossoming of Petrarch in the fifteenth century, Italy had been seeing life anew. Galileo was child of this awakening. The impulse behind him was the Wonder of an open mind at the mechanism of the universe. Two things in the world are ever miraculous—thought and motion.

After the death of the dark age, the European world awoke in the Italian Renaissance to a sense of the Wonders of human thought—their own keen speculation and the marvels of the rediscovered thought of the ancient world. Then imperceptibly, the Things thought of displaced the thought of the thinking, and motion, form, movement, held the attention of men and the genius of Galileo. Something of the same thing has happened in our day; the schools have long studied Human Thought in literature, logic, and speculation. Today has come attention to the more neglected wonders of the Things round us and the technique of the world. With eye and imagination thus fixed on the mystery of motion in falling body and whirling earth and moving star, Galileo started to know, to observe, to prove, to dream.

In so doing he met the Opposition—the obstacles that ever block the way of the man who proposes in thought or deed, something New. First it took the cruder and uglier form of jealousy. We tell but half a truth to young men and women when we say: do well and you will be successful. They are apt to interpret success in term of the world's applause and it is not true that the world ever applauds well-doing. In his own *alma mater,* the ancient University of Pisa, Galileo did well as student and professor of physics at the early age of twenty-five. But his new teachings offended a man. If that man had been an ordinary mortal, it might not have mattered; but he was Giovanni de' Medici, prince of a princely house, and in three short years, at the very outset of his career, Galileo was out of a job. A year later he was called to the University of Padua and finally to Florence itself. The students of all Europe flocked to him, and his inventions and discoveries spread his fame. And as his fame rose, so rose the jealous opposition.

And now men said, not that he offended man, but that he blasphemed God. Blasphemy, heresy, transgression of the dogma of the Catholic Church, were serious things in the sixteenth century. They meant disgrace, poverty, persecution, and death if known and proven. At first then, the thing was whispered as jealous rumor; then it swelled to an open war of pamphlets and books; sermons were preached and formal denouncement of the heretic was made. The Holy Office, which we know as the Inquisition—that dark and cruel child of the Reformation, with its servant the Society of Jesus—took up the matter, and finally the opposition culminated in a summons to Rome and trial before seven Cardinal princes of the Holy Catholic Church.

Such was the Impulse and such the Opposition. Whither was the Path—the way through which Galileo pursued his journey to the End? When the man who has a clear vision of Right, finds himself successfully approaching the goal, how shall he meet Jealousy, Error, Selfishness, and Ignorance? The world has given many answers to this, perhaps the greatest moral problem that rises. Tonight I have to tell the answer that Galileo Galilei gave: For fifty years

> he hesitated;
> he explained to his friends;
> he conciliated his enemies;
> he promised to cease;
> he argued;
> and finally at the age of seventy
> *he lied*—

he, deliberately and with full knowledge publicly and unequivocally, made one of the straightest and most uncompromising denials of what he knew to be the truth, ever recorded and, as the legend is, sealed that falsehood by a whispered statement that he knew he was lying.

I am at present neither defending nor condemning Galileo. I am simply stating the case, and showing you the way in which a man whose service to humanity is unquestioned chose to save his life. For a long time Galileo had been successful in dodging the main issue, namely, does the doctrine that the sun is the center of our universe contradict the Bible? He was full seventy years of age when he was finally brought to trial. It was an imposing sight: on the rear wall of a room in the great palace of the Vatican rose the soft outlines of a famous fresco by Raphael. Before it stretched a long, crimson-coated table. Here sat the prelates of the church in their gorgeous robes—the bishops of seven seas, the princes of the greatest human organization in modern times. A golden crucifix adorned one end and the other held seven golden candlesticks with their lighted tapers. Before the table stood two scarlet cardinals, and a corsetted soldier with drawn sword. In the midst knelt Galileo— a little old man of seventy years, decrepit, and half blind. With palsied hands and trembling lips he said these words:

I, Galileo Galilei, of the age of seventy, being on my knees in the presence of you, most eminent and most reverend Lord Cardinals of the Universal Christian Commonwealth, having before my eyes the holy Gospels, on which I now lay my hands, swear that I have always believed, and now believe, and God helping, that I shall for the future always believe, whatever the Holy Catholic and Apostolic Roman Church holds, preaches, and teaches. But because this Holy Office had enjoined me by precept, entirely to relinquish the false dogma which maintains that the Sun is the center of the world and immovable, and that the Earth is not the center, and moves; not to hold, defend, or teach by any means, or by writing, the aforesaid false doctrine.

Therefore, being willing to take out of the minds of your eminences, and of every Catholic Christian, this vehement suspicion, of right conceived against me, I with sincere heart, and faith unfeigned, abjure, execrate, and detest the aforesaid errors and heresies, and generally every sect contrary to the above-said Holy Church; and I swear that I will nevermore hereafter say or assert, by speech or writing, anything through which the like suspicion may be had of me; but if I shall know anyone heretical, or suspected of heresy, I will denounce him to this Holy Office, or to the Inquisitor and Ordinary of the place in which I shall be. I moreover swear and promise, that I will fulfill and observe entirely all the penitences which have been imposed upon me, or which shall be imposed by this Holy Office. But if it shall happen that I shall go contrary (which God avert) to any

of my words, promises, protestations, and oaths, I subject
myself to all the penalties and punishments, which, by
the Holy Canons, and other Constitutions, general and
particular, have been enacted and promulgated against
such delinquents: So help me God, and his Holy Gospels,
on which I now lay my hands.

Thus he spoke, but as he rose from his knees some say he
whispered, "but it does move." Nine years later the blind and
aged sufferer after long imprisonment and torture, died.[1]

Students and graduates of Fisk University, let us judge this
man: on the one hand range his service to mankind: his discovery of the great laws of motion in the solar system, and on
the other, place the cowardice of his lie; on the one hand the
advantage of a mechnical knowledge of the universe and on the
other the necessity of faith in one's fellow-men as the foundation stone of society. Which is the greatest? Which is the sorest
wound to human progress—the loss of a valuable body of knowledge or the voluntary misdirection of human faith? A blow at
the upbuilding of Truth or a blow at its very foundations?

Science is a great and worthy mistress, but there is one
greater and that is Humanity which science serves; one thing
there is greater than knowledge and that is the Man who
knows. In the midst then of society whose life blood is faith,
and in the name of Science which will know the truth that
the truth may make it free, the verdict of civilization must be
that not even the splendor of the service of Truth done by
Galileo Galilei can wipe away the blot of his cowardly lie. By
that lie, civilization was halted, science was checked, and
bigotry was more strongly enthroned on its crimson glory. And
for what? To aid the discovery of truth? No, for Galileo's great
work was done twenty years before he was tried for his life.
No, it was for the sake of nine years of pitiable blindness and
suffering for an aged and broken man who did not dare to die

1. For a different version of the Galileo contest with the Vatican,
see Giorgio de Santillana, *The Crime of Galileo* (Chicago: University of Chicago Press, 1955).

for the glory of a great cause and make it thus more glorious in his courageous death.

Nor did he lack example. Only forty-three years before his birth, a German monk had faced Christendom for one principle and cried when they shrieked, "Retract"—not *I will not,* but "I *cannot* do otherwise." In the midst of Galileo's young manhood, right there in Rome, Giordano Bruno almost the very same age of Galileo, a defender of the same Copernican system, and unswerving searcher for truth, suffered himself to be burned alive after seven years in prison, rather than to lend himself to a lie to the glory of the Church.

Did it pay? Was the truth worth a lie? Which was the fool, Bruno or Galileo? I know that in this my judgment I speak today to ears that hear faintly and to hardening hearts. And with reason, for I speak to an age that differs from and at the same time resembles Galileo's. His age was beginning to see and sense and appreciate the rhythm of Things—the miracle of motion, the sweep of space and the dominion of matter; we today emerge from a century steeped in the awe and worship of Matter, triumphant in its mastery, insolent in its prophesy. Despite our strongest endeavors a shade of contempt for mere thought and theorizing, for feelings, emotions, and principles tinges our culture and our life. Two miracles the world holds, as I have said: Thought and Motion; and the Age of Thought, which was the age before Galileo, forgets the miracle of Motion; and the Age of Motion, which is our age, condemns the miracle of Thought. Yet above contempt and neglect sweep both, as the ultimate Wonder of Life and woe to the world that blasphemes them.

Today and on us the pressure is tremendous. What is the world, cries the present Philosophy? It is the growing of grain and the weaving of cloth, the moving of wheels and the building of walls; it is the ability to do, the earning of livelihood, the creation of wealth. And then by natural logic this doctrine advances and says, if this is Life, train men for life in natural ways: not by Latin and Greek, but by arithmetic and mechanics. Is this philosophy false? No, but almost as dangerous, for it is half-true. As one-sided as the world that stood in judgment over Galileo and said: With the Bible of God and the Logic of Aristotle to read, what else is there worth studying in the world? The influence of this dogmatism has lasted until our day. There can be no doubt that the college curriculum of the past generation shamefully neglected the World of Things—the tangible visible universe and its laws and ways. It is certain that in the university of tomorrow, the field of knowledge will include a knowledge of what the present world has done and is doing with its physical resources as well as a knowledge of its Thoughts and feelings. For this momentous change in curriculum, all true educators are looking and preparing; but this does not mean a stampede to industry as a substitute for life—to mechanics as an antidote for thought, or to technique in place of Reason.

Simply because in the world of education, we are fighting for change and larger fulfillment of true prophesy, does not mean that any industrializing of a college curriculum, or any substitution of hands for brains, is the true heralded change. For it may easily happen (and this is the gist of my message) that a mere specious and popular promise of longer and easier life, may prompt the Galilean spirit of 1908, as it did in 1608, to seek to establish the mechanical success of the future building by tearing down the spiritual foundations of the past.

Many men would argue in judging Galileo: Are not the laws of Motion worth a lie? Is not the support of a great Negro college worth some deception or surrender? But the Spirit of the Ages answers, No. The foundations which Galileo's lie threatened, were of more infinitely difficult building and perfecting than the great discoveries he made were worth. In travail of soul and gushing of blood; in anger, hatred, sorrow, and strife; in the rise and crash of empires, from Egypt and Babylonia to beautiful Greece and imperial Rome—on all this was the world-Kingdom of Law and Order and Truth raised. They only can speak lightly of the change from the time when each man flew at every one's throat, to that when we safely look for Universal Peace among all nations—they only lightly pass that vision by who never knew of the raging billows of sorrow and blood through which this world has staggered to this goal.

Which is greater, the discovery of the telephone or of universal suffrage? That man is mad who hesitates to answer. So then when a man offers a discovery for a lie, or Education for a bribe, then must the watchman on the outer wall cry Halt— In the King's name!

And you graduates of Fisk University, are the watchmen on the outer wall. And you Fisk University, Intangible but real Personality, builded of Song and Sorrow, and the Spirits of Just Men made perfect, are as one standing Galileo—wise before the Vision of Death and the Bribe of the Lie. Not that I for a moment suppose that anyone now in authority here proposes any decisive change in the attitude or meaning of this University. But the personality of an institution is a peculiar thing. The apparently isolated—almost unconscious movements of individuals, guided by the outside pressure of powerful interests, easily bring that to pass of which they themselves had not dreamed. And so today this venerable institution stands before its problem of future development, with the bribe of Public Opinion and Private Wealth dangling before us, if we will either deny that our object is the highest and broadest training of Black Men, or if we will consent to call Higher Education that which you know and I know is not Higher Education. And I say we, in this case advisedly; for my brothers and sisters, if this happens: if the ideal is lowered or the lie told, the responsibility rests on us. We are the University—we on whose brow it has laid immortal hands, who wear its sign and seal upon our forehead. For us the trustees hold this property; as our representatives these teachers teach. If this republic of letters suffers harm, the guilt lies on us and on our children's children.

Three gifts a graduate may bring back to his Alma Mater— a gift of Gold, and surely today this is needed, for more and more the burden of Negro education is destined on Negro shoulders, and the support of a college like this will eventually come from its alumni. Yet the gift of Gold is not possible to us all, not is it the greatest gift. The second and greater gift is the gift of Accomplishment—of things done, success achieved, knowledge advanced and fostered. Too little of this proof of our training have we brought to Fisk, but a full glorious return did Galileo make to Pisa. Yet this is not the greatest and in making the Greater Gift, this man missed and marred the greatest. For the greatest gift that a scholar can bring to Learning is Reverence of Truth, a Hatred of Hypocrisy and Sham, and an absolute sincerity of purpose. And if after twenty years, we of the class of '88 return with little gold, with but pitiable accomplishment—God grant we bring to this altar, the incense of clean hands and unbending devotion to what we know is the Truth.

First of all then, the thing for which we stand must be clear. We are not opposing industrial education. The vocational training of children is one of the greatest and most promising movements of modern days. But the place for that kind of training is not the College department of Fisk University. To do this would be like using a surgeon's knife for chopping wood. The world needs wood but it has axes for cutting it. There are good and deserving schools for trade teaching. There are but two or three colleges. These colleges are devoted to higher training and they must not be diverted from it. But it may be asked are not technical and mechanical courses of study possible subjects of higher training? They are. The college course of the future is going to be enriched by the inclusion of many courses based on the technique of modern industry and the physical properties of matter. But that does not mean that every part of such knowledge is fit for the college curriculum. The milking of cows is a worthy industry but it is not a cultural study upon which any honest college can base its bachelor's degree. On the other hand the great chemical and physical laws which underlie the making of many food products are matters which could profitably be treated in a college course. And the decision as to the adaptability of certain lines of thought or bodies of knowledge is not a thing to be arrived at by majority vote or racial prejudices, but is a matter of expert study.

If Fisk University wants to know what technical and engineering subjects are fittest to a college course—there are in the United States, France, and Germany, hundreds of universities and other institutions of the very highest standing, whose curricula have been matters of thought, study, and development among the best educational philosophers of the world; learn of these and copy their courses and hold their standards. But if, on the other hand, the standards of a great Negro college are to be set by schools of lower and different object, whither are the ideals of this University falling? If you find that you cannot give technical courses of college grade, then give high-school courses or kindergarten courses and call them by their right names. There may often be excuse for doing things poorly in this world, but there is never any excuse for calling a poorly done thing, well done—of denominating a series of lessons in the training of servants, a course in mechanical engineering.

You will, I am sure, pardon this frank warning and exhortation. The times are perilous. A stubborn determination at this time on the part of the Negro race, to uphold its ideals, keep its standards, and unceasingly contend for its rights, means victory; and victory a great deal sooner than any of you imagine. But a course of self-abasement and surrender, of lowering of ideals and neglecting of opportunity—above all, a philosophy of lying in word or deed for the sake of conciliation or personal gain, means indefinite postponement of the true emancipation of the Negro race in America, for the simple reason that such a race is not fit to be freed.

High above the yellow marbles of Florence glistening among the shining olive leaves seems to hang the ancient Church of the Holy Cross. Below it winds the yellow Arno past Pisa to the azure of the Midland Sea; and beyond the sea lies Africa. Once in the past the surging billows tossed a Florentine barque aloft on the thunders of a storm. All seemed lost in the purple blackness of the night: with wild voices the sailors prayed to all the Saints of Florence, till suddenly one cried, "A vision, a vision: The Holy Cross," and pointed far aloft where seemed to gleam the marble splendor of the Florentine Church. They whirled the ship toward it; it leapt and dashed itself to death on the black and beetling rocks full fifty miles from where, in far off Florence, the Church of the Holy Cross raised silently its towers to God. And beneath these towers slept and sleep the bones of Galileo Galilei.

ENVOY

The repercussions of this speech were immediate. President Merrill resigned in the summer.[2] I was sorry for that. I did not mean this for a personal attack. I was attacking a system and a tendency. The professor of mathematics was dropped in the fall, and the "Department of Applied Sciences" disappeared in 1909. In 1910, Booker Washington joined the Board of Trustees and remained a member until his death in 1915. But he was not active and brought no additional funds to Fisk. It was many years before the philanthropy of the North was willing to support higher education among Negroes with anything like generosity. From 1908 until 1925 Fisk had a severe struggle for existence. Perhaps one cause of this was my speech.

2. The contemporary press—Black and white—seems not to have reported the 1908 Du Bois confrontation with the Fisk authorities. Examination of such publications in Nashville, Chicago, New York, Washington turned up nothing. The *Indianapolis Freeman*—a Booker T. Washington newspaper—did report, in one paragraph on page 6 of its issue dated August 1, 1908, that "Dr. J. G. Merrill, president of Fisk University, Nashville, Tenn., tendered his resignation recently as president of that institution." The story praised his services, and stated that the resignation was due to "ill health."

The Rev. Dr. J. G. Merrill (1840–1920) wrote to Du Bois from his home in South Norwalk, Connecticut, June 30, 1908: " . . . I have resigned as President of Fisk University and my resignation has been accepted." He added that he was a poor collector of money and had several times stated this to the Board of Trustees. He felt that Du Bois's speech was "unwarranted by the real state of the case" and added that the aim of the new department "was to be abreast with the times in which we are living" (Du Bois Papers, in custody of the editor). In his posthumously published *Autobiography* (New York: International Publishers, 1968), p. 130, Du Bois places this event, mistakenly, in 1898; the present editor failed to catch this error in editing that volume.

The College-bred Community [1]

1910

*It was the last year of my first sojourn in Atlanta
University where I had taught for thirteen years.
Academically our success in these days was marked. Our
graduates were among the best teachers of Negroes in
the South; principals of schools and professors in
colleges. Tuskegee without their assistance could not
have kept its doors open. They were beginning to enter
the professions. Their careers and those of their fellows
as shown by our initial study of the college-bred Negro
was remarkable and encouraging. We had begun at
Atlanta University the first systematic study of the
American Negro made anywhere in the world; and yet
Atlanta University was starving to death. Its support, its
funds were dwindling. It had continually to retrench. It
was threatened with debt. Dr. Bumstead, the calm,
hardworking apostle of the Negro college of the day,
was giving his whole life to collecting funds and once
in a while I left my teaching to go North to help him.
On a certain occasion I spoke to the white, rich, and
well-born in Brookline, Massachusetts, and tried to
impress upon them not simply the use, but the
indispensable need of the college-bred man in the South.
I was speaking no longer with the magnificent
confidence of young manhood or the harsh criticism of
mature years, but as a social scientist and observer
convinced of my facts.*

Atlanta University is primarily a college. To be sure
it has a large high school connected with it and an efficient

1. In the original publication of this address, the title is College-
Bred Negro Communities. On the inside back-cover is a direct appeal from the university for funds; it is dated February 1910.

31

normal school; but the students in the normal school are all of college rank, and the high school is retained because there are no public high schools in Georgia for black folk. The center, therefore, of our work in Atlanta University is the College. To the up-building of this department our chief energies are directed; by the results of this department our work must be judged; and on the basis of this department we ask the support of the philanthropic world. Probably no other institution in the world is so entirely a Negro college as ours and certainly none in the South has as large a proportion of college students. We are, then, primarily a college. When, now, this statement is frankly made, there are a great many people who wish to help good causes in the world, who wish us well, and who with equal frankness decline to contribute to our work. They say plainly, "we are not interested in giving black boys college training. We think that the class of Negroes who have reached the plane where they can profit by such higher training have also reached the plane where they do not need outside aid. Such people, white or black, can be left to themselves to make their own way in the world." They say, "we are interested in the submerged classes of those poor people who are struggling up out of the depths. Such people we want to help, but, on the other hand, while theoretically we would be glad to help all people to a broader vision, yet on account of limited ability we are obliged to confine ourselves to cases of pressing necessity; therefore, we cannot give to Negro college work." If, now, the assumption thus stated be true, I would not only not blame philanthropists for refusing to support Atlanta University, but I would go further and change my own work; because the work which lies nearest my heart is not that of the talented few in opposition to the needs of the submerged many. But I have come here tonight purposely to set before you argument which proves to me, and I trust will prove to you, that the assumption which I mention is false, and that the first step toward lifting the submerged mass of black people in the South is through the higher training of the talented few.[2]

2. Omitted here is the following paragraph that appears in the

There are many of us who are still surprised, not to say indignant, that it took ten years of Reconstruction even to begin the settlement of the problems raised by slavery and war. Such people strongly suspect that only the incompetence and rascality of the Reconstruction politicians can explain such an extraordinary fact. And yet, when we come to consider the matter, how few of us realize what slavery meant in the South! To kidnap a nation; to transplant it in a new land, to a new language, new climate, new economic organization, a new religion and new moral customs; to do this is a tremendous wrenching of social adjustments; and when society is wrenched and torn and revolutionized, then, whether the group be white or black, or of this race or that, the results are bound to be far reaching.

When, therefore, you say that the South had a system of slavery for 250 years, you mean that the victims of that system lost their own social heritage; gained new bonds binding them to a new community, and began to forge in that new community, new machinery for carrying on the new social life; or, in other words, religion, moral customs, family life, economic habits, literature and traditions were taken from the Africans. They became a part of a rigid caste system, out of which they could seldom legally rise, and their social organization among themselves was reduced to the barest minimum for existence.

When, after two and one-half centuries of storm and stress, the race was adjusted to these new social environments, there came abruptly a new revolution. That revolution ushered them into what was called freedom; the social heritage and the bonds which tied them to their community were again broken, and they were left with no machinery for carrying on

---

original: "The truth of this proposition is less obvious because college training is not of the same necessity in the North, and the arguments for it do not rest upon the same premises, as in the South among black people; nor is reason for this far to seek. The study of social development is still so young and so inchoate that it is difficult for us to think in terms of its obvious teaching."

their social life. Or again, to make the matter more explicit, the Negro was freed after he had lost much of his own native traditions and moral and economic habits and had only begun to learn other habits from his master. Moreover, as a freedman, it was made increasingly impossible for him to learn such things from his masters because he was separated more and more from the master-class. Thirdly, having forgotten or never known the methods of modern organization, it was quite impossible that he should immediately take up and guide the development of his own institutions.

What, now, was the one great pressing need? Of course this need has been variously expressed and emphasized. To some the first thing that freedom meant was work; to some it was a release from the bonds of poverty; to others it was education and the organization of religious institutions. But yet I think if we consider the matter, all of these reduce themselves to one single thing, looked at from different points of view; namely what the Negro needed was experience, that is, a knowledge of how the world accomplishes its necessary work today. And when you say that the freed Negro was ignorant of this, you mean more than mere illiteracy—for illiteracy is the cause of evils rather than the evil in itself. You mean more than shift-lessness and unmoral customs. In fact, you mean all these things together and other things added, which in the total show that the Negro did not know the accumulated wisdom and methods of the world in which he was asked to take part. Now, how was he to get this unknown experience and wisdom? There were people simple-minded enough to suppose it was a mere matter of teaching him to read and write. I remember meeting a good friend of the race not long since who said with a rather puzzled expression that he "did not understand why all Negroes were not fairly well-educated, since they had had primary schools for a generation." He was doubly wrong; first, because as a matter of fact, not one-third of the Negro children have primary schools.[3] Primary schools are simply one means

3. The original at this point reads as follows: "He was doubly wrong: first, because as a matter of fact, not one-third of the Negro

of making education possible. The chief and great method, of course, by which a people come into the great social heritage of the modern culture-world and by which they gain close and efficient knowledge of the methods of the world's work is the training which comes primarily and essentially from human contact—a contact of those who know with those who are to learn.

Now, the great mistake which some of you and many others make, when they talk and think about the South, is to assume that there are in the South the same facilities for the transmission of culture from class to class and man to man as exist in the North. If this were so, then my argument today would be quite out of place. But I come to emphasize in your minds a thing which you all know; namely, that racial separation in the South means the voluntary and persistent isolation of those who most need to learn by race contact. People who have easily and rather lightly accepted a program of race separation in the South have, I fear, seldom thought of this. In the North, of course, in the last twenty-five years, the development has been exactly in the opposite way: it has been toward greater and more frequent and broader contact of the more favored classes of society with the less favored; a contact not simply in matters of alms-giving and economic organization, but in all of the deeper matters of human interest. The result of this is that Northern people are apt to assume that this same great social movement is in progress in the South, and consequently when there comes from the South word of certain kinds of movements, they assume that these things are in addition to the natural growing contact of the extremes of society. Yet you have but to think a moment to know that this is not true. There is in the South a social separation between workman and employer, the ignorant and the learned,[4] society and its servants, the high and low, white and black, which goes to

---

children have primary schools today; secondly, because you can not educate a people in primary schools."

4. In the original this phrase reads: "the ignorant class and the learned class."

an extent and reaches a degree quite unrealized by those who have not studied the situation.

I pause simply to remind you that white people and black people in the South do not, as a rule, live on the same streets or in the same sections; do not travel together in train or street-car; do not attend the same churches, do not listen to the same lectures, do not employ the same physicians, do not go to the same schools; do not, for the most part, work at the same kinds of work; do not read the same books and papers, are not taught the same traditions, and are not buried in the same graveyard.

Now, outside of all questions of the wisdom or necessity for such a situation, the question which interests us today is this: how far and in what way can there be any transmission of human culture and experience or knowledge of social organization and social methods or of education, in any sense, from the white group to the black? Of course, some such transmission there is and always will be—it is impossible perfectly to isolate people; but the chance of such transmission is in the South reduced to a minimum.

Mind, I make no argument for or against racial separation. But I am saying, with emphasis: state in your own mind, every argument for racial isolation at its full strength; conclude, if you will, that my child shall not be educated with yours; that it is indiscreet to eat [with me] at the same table; that you have definite matrimonial plans for your sister [which do not include me];[5] and that black people and white cannot righteously worship God from the same pews. Assert these beliefs, either for yourselves or in sympathy with others who passionately insist upon them, and then remember that the stronger this argument is for racial isolation, the more compelling is the righteous demand of black folk for their own racial leadership, their own fountains of knowledge, their own centers of culture; and this is not for their amusement or delectation; not to flatter their vanity, but to give them the absolute and

5. The words bracketed by the editor do not occur in the original printed version.

indispensable foundation for solid and real advance in civilization and social reform, the uplifting of their masses, and rational guidance in health, work, and morals.

If, then, you propose to educate the Negro into the possibility of full citizenship in the modern world of culture, one thing you have got to admit at the very outset; and that is, he cannot, to any appreciable extent, get that education from the white people about him. Now, this is true, on the whole, of no other constituent part of the American people. If higher college training is asked for poor American boys, for Armenians, or for white mountainers, it is sufficiently just to say there is at present a more crying need for certain forms of elementary training among these boys than for college training. Their guidance and training in the higher matters of social evolution can be safely left to the result of their contact with the best of their fellow citizens. But with the Negro this is not true. By the silent decree of the nation he is, in the South, shut off and isolated. And much of this program is being easily accepted in the North.

What the Negro needs, therefore, of the world and civilization, he must largely teach himself; what he learns of social organization and efficiency, he must learn from his own people. His conceptions of social uplift and philanthropy must come from within his own ranks, and he must above all make and set and follow his own ideals of life and character. Now, this is putting upon a people just emerged from slavery, with neither time, traditions, nor experience, a tremendous task. In strict justice, it is asking more of this people than the American nation has any right to ask. Nevertheless, this race is not stopping to await justice in this matter; it is not asking about the righteousness of past conduct; it is not even pausing—as perhaps it ought—to discuss the advisability of present policies; but it is asking you, here and now, to place in its hands the indispensable facilities for teaching itself those things which it must know if it is going to share modern civilization.

Moreover, just as in justice you cannot ask a man to raise himself by his own boot-straps, just so you cannot logically and justly expect that a people will furnish itself, under such circumstances, with its own chief means of uplift. The natural temptation for a group in our situation is to look around them upon their neighbors, pick out that which in their inexperience seems to be the cause of success and, advancing and seizing it lightly, try to march on. If the thing which they choose is momentarily popular they will receive for choosing it exaggerated applause; just as they were applauded in 1868 for political acumen because politics were popular, just so today they are applauded for showing signs of industrial shrewdness, because industry is the ruling movement today. Now, both politics and industry are the leading and main foundations of every successful state, but the great point is that any people to be successfully civilized must know how to handle those great tools of advance, and they can only learn this from a knowledge of the world's experience through the teaching of a cultured class.

The *community* must be able to take hold of its individuals and give them such a social heritage, such present social teachings and such compelling social customs as will force them along the lines of progress, and not into the great forests of death. What is needed then, for any group of advancing people, is the COLLEGE-BRED COMMUNITY; for no matter how far the college may fail in individual cases, it is, after all, the center where knowledge of the past connects with the ideal of the future. Every community, therefore, must be *college-bred*; and that does not mean that every individual must be a college graduate; it may be that the proportion of college-bred men may be small, even infinitesimal; and still the community, by tradition and heritage, will hold fast to what the past has taught the world of high and ideal future accomplishment. But, given a group or community which does not know the message of the past and does not have within its own number, the men who can feel it, and is separated from contact with outside groups who can teach it—given such a community and you have a desperate situation, which calls for immediate remedy. It is such a situation among the Negroes in the South that calls for schools like Atlanta University.

There ought to be in the South today at least five institutions with an endowment of a million dollars each, whose business it would be to furnish the teachers and professional men and thinkers and industrial leaders for the masses of the black people of the South. Such colleges would represent, not the capstone of the social organization of the South but rather its vast foundation. As a matter of fact, such institutions today, tremendously hampered as they are in their work, have, nevertheless, begun this work of giving communities college training and have so far, done remarkably well. To them is due the establishment of the Negro school system in the South with 21,000 teachers; the establishment and conduct of the great and efficient industrial schools; the development and guidance to a considerable extent of the 35,000 Negro churches and the accumulation personally and through their influence of the more than $650,000,000 worth of Negro wealth. It would, of course, be wrong to say that Negro colleges were responsible for every step which the black man has taken in advance since the war; but it is not too much to say that but for the black men trained in the colleges North and South, and the students who were in turn trained by them, the major part of this progress would have been utterly impossible. Moreover, it is not simply in education that the Negro college accomplishes its mission of human culture. Nearly all the adjuncts by which culture is diffused in the North have been absent among Negroes in the South: the public lecture and public library; the sympathetic newspaper, organized charity, and social settlements; the Young Men's Christian Association and Women's Clubs, etc. Today, all these instruments of culture are making their appearance slowly but surely, and they are coming directly from the Negro colleges and from centers of influence where the graduates of such colleges are working. The COLLEGE-BRED COMMUNITY, therefore, in the South is already beginning to be a reality, but it needs tremendous reinforcement and continual impulse.

In the North the ordinary boy, whether he actually attends college or not, gets some college training from his surroundings. It is impossible for a boy to grow up here in Boston without getting from the air which he breathes something of that for which Harvard stands. On the other hand it is possible for a black boy to grow up in the South and be a perfect barbarian. It is for you and me to make this more and more impossible in the future by giving such support to the best of the Negro colleges as will really plant ideals of social efficiency and culture in the center of black communities and enable them to work and save and act according to the best traditions of civilized men.

To the existence of such group development and feeling among black men there can be but one objection, and that is the objection of those people who mean by "race separation" not separation but subordination; who plainly and frankly say that the Negro is to be separated from all contact with culture in order that he may never become an efficient, self-reliant, thinking race; who hope that there shall grow up in the nation, not the democracy dreamed of by the Pilgrim Fathers but a new caste ideal such as was made the cornerstone of the Confederacy. With such objections I am sure you have no sympathy and I only hope that with your willing desire to help the lowly of all races and peoples, you will use this method of approaching the problem of the submerged mass in a particular race, and through a Negro college, in a larger sense, you will be willing to help a people to help themselves.

ENVOY

To these and similar speeches of mine and appeals of Dr. Bumstead and others, there was some, but not great response. Between 1910 and 1925 the case of college training for Negroes in the South became desperate. I began to feel that one of the reasons that Atlanta University did not get funds was my presence and I therefore accepted a chance to change my scientific career to a career of propaganda in New York with the Nation Association for the Advancement of Colored People, as editor of the Crisis.

Diuturni Silenti

From 1910 to 1924, I was out of direct touch with Negro education. There came the world of war during which I had sent my daughter to Bedales School in England, thinking the war would be short. She was forced to come home in 1914, and went to the Brooklyn Girls' High School. She did not like it. The teaching methods, and the atmosphere were strange to her. She stuck it out and graduated, but was indifferent to a college course. It occurred to me that she might be as thrilled as I once was, if she went south to Fisk. I applied for admission after she was graduated from high school and there was some rather curious and to me inexplicable hesitation, but she was finally admitted. She seemed happy there. She made no complaints. Yet there filtered through certain criticisms of the Fisk of 1924, and once when I was visiting there a student came to me, slipping up almost furtively in the twilight.

It was my first talk with George Streator, then a junior. He said to me: "Don't you want to know what is going on at Fisk?" Afterward I opened my ears. I listened, wrote and investigated, and I was astonished at a state of affairs of which I had not dreamed. When I complained to my daughter for not telling me of conditions, she answered placidly: "I thought you knew!" The student discipline at Fisk had retrograded so as to resemble in some respects a reform school. The administration of the school seemed based on organized gossip. The desperate attempt to get funds had led to a surrender to Southern sentiment compared to which the overtures of Dr. Merrill were but faint and unimportant. The spirit of the school seemed wrong and from time to time teachers, students, and graduates appealed to me.

41

*Again it was the date of one of my continually
reoccurring reunions. In 1923, I had been graduated
thirty-five years. I had not spoken that year because my
daughter was graduating the next year; and so in 1924
I came to Fisk University determined to do an
unpleasant duty and do it thoroughly. I determined to
voice the widespread criticism of alumni, students, and
friends of Fisk University at the way in which the
president, trustees, and faculty were conducting the
school and I was going to do it at Fisk, face to face with
its officials. And so in the Memorial Chapel with my
back to the great organ and with the president and his
wife sitting in front of me and the alumni ranged row on
row, while the undergraduates looked down from the
gallery in suspense, I literally "lifted my voice and
taught them saying":*

You who have not wholly forgotten your Latin, will remember that the two words of my subject are taken from the
beginning of Cicero's oration in defense of Marcellus. I recall
the stilted translation thereof which I committed to memory in
my boyhood:

> To my long continued silence, Conscript Fathers, which
> I have made use of in these days, not on account of any
> fear, but partly from grief, partly from shame, this day
> brings an end and also a beginning of my speaking
> according to my former custom what I think and what I
> know.

To make these perhaps somewhat cryptic words more clear to
you, may I say a few words concerning my connection with Fisk
University. I was graduated from Fisk thirty-six years ago this
month after three years of splendid inspiration and nearly perfect happiness, under teachers whom I respected and amid surroundings that inspired me. I regarded the ten years after my
graduation from 1888 to 1898 simply as a sort of prolongation
of my Fisk college days. I was at Harvard but not of it. I was a

student of Berlin, but still the son of Fisk; and I came back to Fisk to deliver the commencement address in 1898[1] and to make that address a welcome to my younger fellows into the high calling of those who had gone forth from this institution with fine determination and splendid inspiration.

Ten other years passed and when I returned here as alumni speaker in 1908, there was a shadow as it seemed to me already across this institution. The trend toward industrial education was to my mind beginning to lower the standards and vitiate the ideals for higher college training which were the heritage of Fisk University. I spoke my complaint clearly and sought to warn this institution that it would never do, for purposes of expediency, to lie to the world as Galileo once lied when he knew that his heart held the truth. This speech of mine was received with much criticism, and from that time to this, sixteen years, I have not been invited to speak at this institution. Once or twice when I happened of necessity to be on the grounds I have been invited to say a few words and have made perfunctory remarks knowing that nothing further was expected. I knew too that my thoughts and ideals were distasteful to those from whom Fisk at this time was expecting financial aid, and as I had neither money nor monied friends I took refuge in silence even when I sensed wrong.

Today I recognize that my invitation to address the alumni is largely a matter of circumstances and not of deliberate choice on the part of this institution. Nevertheless I have come to address you and, I say frankly, I have come to criticize. I have known and been connected more or less intimately with many colored institutions of learning, but I have never known an institution whose alumni on the whole are more bitter and disgusted with the present situation in this university than the alumni of Fisk University today. This, of course, is not true of all the alumni, but it is true of so great and so important a part that Fisk University ought to know it.

I have come therefore to criticize and to say openly and be-

1. See item 3 in the Bibliography.

fore your face what so many of your graduates are saying secretly and behind your back. I maintain that the place to criticize Fisk University is at Fisk University and not elsewhere; and above all I maintain that this is the time and the critical time in the history of this institution when the opinion of its alumni and constituents must be known and decision must be taken by the trustees and faculty as to the future policy of Fisk University. And it is for this reason that I say: "To my long continued silence, Conscript Fathers, which I have made use of in these days, not on account of any fear, but partly from grief, partly from shame, this day brings an end and also a beginning of my speaking according to my former custom, what I think and what I know."

I come to defend two theses, and the *first* is this: *Of all the essentials that make an institution of learning, money is the least.* The *second* is this: *The alumni of Fisk University are and of right ought to be, the ultimate source of authority in the policy and government of this institution.*

Taking up the first thesis I do not, of course, mean for a moment to be so foolish as to say that a university does not need money. Fisk University does need money; any institution needs today physical equipment, buildings, laboratories, and salaries and needs them imperatively; and yet I do maintain that this equipment is not the greater need. I maintain that there is a spiritual equipment, without which no institution can really exist as a center of culture, and I trust that it will never be necessary to say of Fisk University as was once said of Brown University: "Yesterday Brown University had a president; today it has a million dollars."

Three great things are necessary for the spiritual equipment of an institution of learning: *Freedom of Spirit, Self-Knowledge,* and a recognition of the *Truth*. These are trite phrases, but they are none-the-less eternally true; and *first* of all comes Freedom of Spirit.

It is a beautiful figure that we continually use in depicting the relationship of college and student; Alma Mater—Fostering Mother. We see always in this true relationship the arm of this

44   Diuturni Silenti

old mother about the shoulders of her sons and grandsons and grandsons' grandsons, whispering to their ears. "Behold the beautiful land which the Lord thy God has given thee!" And nowhere is this inspiration needed more than in the case of colored students today. They come out of the Valley of the Shadow with souls that have been hurt and crushed, and the great duty of the Negro college is to say to these students that the little sordid things of earth and of ordinary life where they lack so much freedom, are as nothing compared with the great free realm of the spirit.

I have often told audiences of my experience when I went first to see the Bernese Oberland. I stood on the plaza of the cathedral at Berne and looked upon the Alps. I saw the great green hills and rising mountains. They were fine and I was glad. I started to turn away, and then, almost by accident, I lifted my eyes up to the sky, and there, above the hills and above the mountains, up where I had thought of nothing but mists and clouds, blazed in unearthly splendor the snow-capped Alps—sublime, magnificent. And so it is with these colored students. It is inspiration and light and the free, untrammeled spirit that rises above the earth which they seek in college. Through this very freedom comes discipline, and through discipline comes freedom.

What now is Fisk University doing to uphold and to spread the spirit of freedom in this institution? It is not doing what it should. In Fisk today, discipline is choking freedom; threats are replacing inspiration, iron-clad rules, suspicion, tale bearing are almost universal. A favorite expression is, "if you don't like Fisk University, get out!" If you do not agree with all the policies of the institution, go elsewhere. Students are made to promise in writing not simply to obey the rules of the institution but to obey *all future rules that may be made*. Even during my short stay of a few days, I have seen crass instances of discipline. At the senior chapel, the last, and as it should have been, holiest exercise, everything was held up for five minutes until the presiding official publicly disciplined a few giggling girls.

Instances of discipline have occurred here, almost criminal

in their miscarriage of justice. I have known a girl to be sent home for theft because she could not satisfactorily explain her possession of a five-dollar bill; and when afterward it was proven beyond a doubt that the money was rightfully hers, no apology was ever made. She was simply told quietly that she could come back. She has since graduated with honor at Howard University. To illustrate in what glaring contrast the present discipline of Fisk University stands with the discipline of my day let me recall one instance.

I was seventeen years old. Perhaps my older class mates were having fun at my expense, but at any rate I was told that at commencement time the ordinary rules did not hold. I consequently walked boldly up through yonder white gates and invited Dickey to take a walk. (She was called Dickey because her father wanted a son and named her Richard anyway.) We sauntered out the front gate in broad day light, down the long path, past Livingston, called at the city home of one of our fellow students, Lizzie Jones, found other students there and danced and ate. Then we walked back in the dying day and came to Jubilee Hall about sunset.

It looked as though the roof of the hall was about to rise. The matron was furious. "But I didn't know that I was breaking any rule," I stammered. I was given to understand that I ought to have known, which did not seem to me a bit logical; and then I came before the president. He was a tall, white-haired man with bushy eyebrows and deep eyes, in the depths whereof always lurked a smile. And he said to me quietly, "don't do it again." And I didn't. He bound me to him for time and eternity by that one wise judgment. He knew perfectly well that if a boy is up to a nasty trick he doesn't walk out of the front gate in full daylight.

I do not for a moment doubt that the objects which Fisk today wishes to gain by her discipline are in themselves perfectly good objects; but the trouble is that she is trying to accomplish her ends by methods which are medieval, and long since discredited. The second and third generation of colored students present their problems of discipline and guidance, but those problems in the long run are no greater than the problems presented everywhere in the training of youth throughout the colleges of the United States and the world; and of all ways of treating these problems and settling them, the method of piling rule on rule and threat on threat is the worst and most ineffective, and it makes not men but hypocrites.

Fisk University wishes to be recognized by the great institutions of learning, and yet at other institutions students are being taught discipline through freedom. When Bertrand Russell was not allowed to speak at Harvard University the students protested not simply to the faculty but to the overseers, and their right to protest was freely recognized. No protest would for a moment be tolerated on the part of the students of Fisk. If a student even feels disagreement with the policies of Fisk he is given to understand that he is not wanted. It is the spirit of freedom that has built the great universities of the world, and Fisk can never be great until it recognizes that spirit. The pall of fear which envelops the student body of this institution is the most awful thing here.

The second great thing that characterizes an institution of learning is *Self-Knowledge,* the principle ancient as Greece and older: "Know Thyself." The students are in college for purposes of self-expression and experiment; to test their own wings, to find ability and strengthen character, to learn self-control. In such self-experience on the part of the young there is a cost to pay, a certain waste that is inevitable; the appearance of youthful swagger and impudence; and yet the wiser world has learned that in youth, even as in age, the Cost of Freedom is less than the Price of Repression. At Fisk University the temptation and the tendency is to cramp self-expression, reduce experiment to the lowest terms and cast everything in an iron mould. College women are put in uniforms in a day when we reserve uniforms for those who are organized to murder, for lackeys and for insane asylums and jails. Not only is the system of uniforms at Fisk ineffective and wasteful, but its method of enforcement is humiliating and silly.

The students are allowed to do almost nothing of their own initiative. They can have no organizations except such as are not simply supervised by the faculty but are in part run by the faculty with membership determined by the faculty, with some long-eared member of the faculty sitting in at every meeting to listen.

There can be no opinion expressed by the students in any public way. If I have any knowledge of the English language and any facility in expression that began with the three years spent on the editorial staff of the *Fisk Herald*. The *Fisk Herald* was for a long time one of the oldest student papers in the United States. It was a shame to suppress it. Other colored institutions even below college grade and practically all white institutions have their student papers. Fisk University is not allowed to have one. Athletics are hampered and threatened with extinction by faculty action.

Thus self-expression and manhood are choked at Fisk in the very day when we need expression to develop manhood in the colored race. We are facing a serious and difficult situation. We need every bit of brains and ability that we have for leadership. There is no hope that the American Negro is going to develop as a docile animal. He is going to be a man, and he needs therefore his best manhood. This manhood is being discouraged at Fisk today and ambition instead of being fostered is being deliberately frowned upon.

I met a young man the other day in an institution far from here. He walked up and stuck out his hand and said, "I am Hunter's son." I remembered Hunter in my college days at Fisk—a big, strong, muscular black man. He got angry once at some of my pert criticism and gripped me. I thought my arm was coming off. These were the days before the legal "Jim Crow" law, but the brakemen used to take it upon themselves to force all colored passengers into the smoking car. Hunter went down with the other students after commencement to board the train. The brakeman barred the way to the passenger coach. Hunter swept the brakeman aside with one arm and with the other beckoned the students. They walked into the coach singing. This was Hunter's son. I looked at him with interest. Why wasn't he at Fisk University? Is Fisk University afraid of men of this sort? Is this the kind of person that she expels for impudence? Is Fisk trying to make the roll of her expulsions a sort of roll of honor? Is she afraid to have these students know themselves?

The third thing that a university stands for is the recognition of *Truth,* the search for Truth. We say this glibly now, but we must remember that in every age while institutions of learning have accepted and taught certain parts of the truth there are other parts about which they have hesitated. For a long time geology could not be taught in our institutions because it interfered with the biblical "six days." Today some people are trying to enjoin the teaching of Evolution; and continually in our day the teaching of the truth concerning our social structure and economic development is being hindered and suppressed. That this is dangerous goes without saying; but the greatest of dangers faces those institutions of the South, white and colored, that are afraid to tell the truth concerning the difficult social environment in which the youth of the South is growing up.

One can imagine, of course, two extreme attitudes which a Negro college might take with regard to the surrounding South; it might teach that the case is hopeless; that no Negro can expect to be a man in this country with the present attitude and determination of the whites. Or it might go to the opposite extreme and say that all is well; that the best thought of the country is tending toward justice and that the Negro's only hindrance is himself. Neither of these positions is tenable. And a real university with honest purpose today ought frankly to face the fact that there are here forces of advancement and uplift, that there are forces of evil and retrogression, and that it is for the educated man to find a way amid these difficulties.

Fisk University is not taking an honest position with regard to the Southern situation. It has deliberately embraced a propaganda which discredits all of the hard work which the forward-looking fighters for Negro freedom have been doing. It overpraises the liberal white South. It continually teaches its students and constituency that this liberal white South is in the ascendency and that it is ruling; and that the only thing required of the black man is acquiescence and submission. Thus the *Fisk News,* speaking without right and without warrant for

Fisk University, for its alumni and its constituency, is advocating and spreading a doctrine which every student in this university knows is dishonest. They know and they appreciate the things which the white friends of humanity living in the South are doing, but they know that these liberal white folk are not triumphant, that they are facing a terrific wall of prejudice and evil; and every day these students in their lives are experiencing this evil. They know "Jim Crow" cars; they know the effects of disfranchisement; they know personal and persistent insult. You cannot teach these children honesty as long as you dishonestly deny these truths which they know all too well.

Let me bring two things to your mind—and I am speaking now not of lawless lynchings and of the mob, but of the acts of Southern white men of the better class. There was a man in south Georgia, a colored man, upon whose land I once stood. He owned ten thousand acres free of debt. He had schools and churches, white tenants and colored tenants. The other day he died without a will and at the request of his inexperienced widow, his friend, the white banker, undertook to settle his estate. In less than a year every cent of this man's property was gone and today his girls are dancing in a cabaret in New York to support themselves and the widowed mother.

Or, to take another phase: In Birmingham, Alabama, the condition of the colored schools has long been a shame. At last in order to get a large bond issue of three million dollars, the best white citizens solemnly promised to spend five hundred thousand dollars upon the Negro schools. They proposed to put up a Negro high school to cost three or four hundred thousand dollars and one large primary school. They had, however, as principal of the colored high school a Negro tool and lickspittle. He assured them that the colored people didn't need any school as costly as they proposed. He asked for a straggling one-story building with a little brick and a great deal of stucco and at a cost of about half what they had proposed to spend. He achieved a partly finished high school. It is precisely such lickspittles and cowards that the propaganda carried on by the *Fisk News* is developing, and it will never be successful because it holds within itself its own contradiction and denial.

The truth concerning the present racial situation is systematically kept from Fisk students as well as the truth concerning the great liberal movements of the world. Representatives of the International Youth Movement complained that Fisk was one of the few American institutions where they were not allowed contact with the students. Representatives of colored fraternities with their "Go to High School, Go to College" campaign were not allowed to speak at Fisk. The National Association for the Advancement of Colored People, which has done more than any organization for the freedom of the Negro race and for making the interracial movement possible, has never been represented at Fisk University. And yet Fisk University pretends to be an institution for the presentation of the truth.

To recapitulate, Fisk University is choking freedom. Self-knowledge is being hindered by refusal of all initiative to the students. Fisk University is not teaching the truth about the race problem.

What is the reason for this state of affairs at Fisk? We colored people, talking among ourselves of the action of white folk toward us continually bring in one general essential cause and that is total depravity—the determination on the part of the white world to do us all possible ill.

Such a reason is, of course, fanciful in nearly all cases, and in this case I do not believe that those in control of Fisk University wish or desire anything but the welfare of the colored race. But the difficulty is that they do not know what is for our good or what we think is for our good. They have not before them facts that are well known to us and points of view and considerations which are to us of tremendous importance. It is in this case, as in so many others, ignorance that leads to evil.

Have you ever seen a king "By the grace of God"? I have. I remember as a young man walking down the *Unter den Linden* from the Royal Palace past the university and toward the Brandenburg Gate. Suddenly there would be a signal and the crowd would turn to the curb and stiffen, standing at attention. Far up the broad avenue came the flash of cream and silver, the waving of plumes, and the prancing of horses; and then he flew by, erect, stern and splendid, *"Wilhelm, von Gottes Gnade, Koenig von Preussen, Deutscher Kaiser."* He has passed today. He was not a bad man, he was a mistaken one. He did not know. He did not call the real German people to council, and he failed because he did not know. And so whenever a man or a group of men assume to rule over others who are separated from them by class or racial or economic interest they are going to make terrible mistakes if the ruled and the rulers do not sit down and take counsel together. The theory of democracy is not that the people have all wisdom or all ability, but it is that the mass of people form a great reservoir of knowledge and information which the state will ignore at its peril.

So in Fisk University. There are at the service of the Trustees, the President, and the Faculty great streams of knowledge and experience; the knowledge and experience of these students here; the knowledge and experience of the whole black world in America which is more and more becoming bound together in organized unity. Fisk University is systematically ignoring these sources of information. It is not consulting the students, it is ordering them about. In only one of the commencement exercises that I have seen did the students have any chance to speak or express themselves, and in that case the President and Faculty were conspicuous by their absence, while the speeches were evidently carefully censored.

In the business which I conduct I pay out over fifty thousand dollars a year; and yet in the fifteen years that I have conducted that business I have never been so threatened with penalties for debt as I have in the last four years in trying to pay my daughter's expenses at Fisk. It was almost impossible, in the first place, to find what sums were due and when they were to be paid; and when finally I did get notice it was almost invariably too late for me to forward a check before the date on which some penalty for nonpayment was due. Several times I have telegraphed funds. And I know of one father, one of the wealthiest graduates of Fisk, whose daughter was publicly denied the right to get books at the book store while across the road at the treasury there lay a balance to her credit. Parents who try to get into sympathetic touch with this institution find no encouragement and those who visit it are usually treated with the scantest courtesy.

The alumni have no voice in the policy or conduct of the institution. They get no communications except a demand for contributions. Almost nothing is done to encourage alumni reunions. No careful record is kept of alumni activities, and while from time to time one or even two alumni are upon the Board of Trustees, they are alumni selected by the President and the Trustees and not by the Alumni Association; and they may or may not represent the opinion of the alumni.

The colored world of Nashville is entirely out of sympathy and out of touch with Fisk University. They attend the exercises held in dwindling numbers. I was present this year at one of the Mozart Society concerts. It was a fine exercise, with excellent singing and some of the greatest colored soloists in America, including Florence Cole Talbert. But the society sang to empty benches. I doubt if there were two hundred people in the chapel. And yet I have known the day when a young black boy from west Tennessee, almost untrained, sang that incomparable tenor solo from *The Messiah*, "Comfort ye, comfort ye, my People," to an audience that covered every inch of the old chapel in Livingston Hall. Today even at the exercises of commencement week there is plenty of room for everybody and sometimes wide empty spaces. The black world of Nashville, and not simply the educated, but the ordinary colored people, know that Fisk University does not want them; that it is straining every effort to attract Southern white people and is segregating and insulting its colored auditors.

Suppose that instead of this attitude the authorities of Fisk University took the trouble to consult their alumni and their constituents and their students. Take, for instance, the matter of clothes. There was once a colored leader who sneered at the pianos in the homes of poor colored people, but it was pointed out to his quick discomfiture that it was a fine thing for the poor to spend on music even that which they might have spent on bread. Did it not show the innate beauty of their souls? And so today Fisk University sneers and raves and passes all sorts of rules against the overdressing of its students, particularly of its women; and there is no doubt but what colored people of the better class waste money in personal adornment. At the same time consider for a moment the reasons: Have you ever ridden on a "Jim Crow" car? I have. I have just come here from riding on many. For the most part they are dirty, ugly, unpleasant. Have you ever been in the colored section of a Southern city? Despite the effort of the colored people to beautify their homes, the city leaves this section as muddy and nasty and unkempt and unprotected as possible. I just looked upon a new graded school in Atlanta. It was the ugliest building I have ever seen. It went out of its way to be ugly. I thought at first it was a factory of the meaner sort.

All through the life of colored people and of their children the world makes repeated efforts to surround them with ugliness. Is it a wonder that they flame in their clothing? that they desire to fill their starved souls with overuse of silk and color? They may fail in their object or overdo it, but now and then they do achieve startlingly fine results. I saw upon the campus this afternoon two girls. (Do not worry, they were not from Fisk University and did not break your rules.) They were dressed in filmy garments with scarfs of crimson and blue about their necks and the setting sun beyond Jubilee Hall threw its glory over them. They were a startlingly beautiful sight. I do not for a moment dispute that the parents of the girls of Fisk University tend to waste money on their clothes; but I do say that New England old maids dressed like formless frumps in dun and drab garments, have no right utterly to suppress and insult these children of the sun even if they want to wear silk; and that to inculcate good taste in dress is a far more subtle matter than stiff rules and harsh judgments.

Consider the matter of fraternities. Fisk University is the only one of the larger colored colleges which does not allow fraternities. There are many sound reasons of this attitude. We know what fraternities have done in the matter of snobbishness and disintegration in many of our large institutions. On the other hand, those institutions have not abolished fraternities and they must have their reasons. Moreover in the case of the colored fraternities their whole inner spirit and the reason for their being differentiates them entirely from white college organizations. They grew up in white northern colleges where colored students were suffering a social ostracism which interfered seriously with their college work. They spread to colored colleges because of the serious efforts which they were making to increase and vivify the college spirit. The "Go to High School, Go to College" campaign carried on annually by the Alpha Phi Alpha fraternity has been one of the greatest incentives in America to push colored youth toward higher education. Not only is that fraternity not allowed in Fisk University, but its representatives could not even come there to speak on the higher education campaign. Another colored fraternity has its "Guide Right" campaign seeking to guide colored graduates into proper employment. The sororities are offering scholarships and prizes to colored graduates. Fisk University has no right autocratically and without consultation with or listening to the advice of students, parents, and alumni to ban these powerful and influential organizations and cut their graduates off from the best fellowship for life.

In northern Ohio there is the city of Cleveland. For fifty years the colored group in Cleveland has fought for municipal recognition and equality and it has accomplished a splendid work. Our great colored author, Charles W. Chesnutt, is a member of one of the leading literary and social clubs. A colored lawyer, Harry Davis, is a member of the Cleveland City Club and long has served in the Ohio Legislature. We have colored councilmen. We have colored teachers in the public schools who teach without segregation or discrimination. There is not a single "Jim Crow" institution in the city, and this is because with fifty years' fighting we have achieved real democracy in Cleveland.

Last year, Fisk University went to Cleveland and arranged a dinner and meeting with influential citizens, at which the President of the Board of Trustees and the President of the University spoke. No colored people were invited or expected. No colored people were consulted as to what ought to be said in that city. The next day the papers reported that Fisk University believed in segregation for colored people and thought it was inevitable and permanent! I am aware that explanations were made afterwards; that the speakers affirmed that they were expressing a fact and not a theory; but the best that can be said of them is that they awkwardly and maladroitly made statements that hurt the cause of the Negro in Cleveland and did the cause of Fisk no good. Suppose that before they staged this meeting they had had a little private talk with their alumni in Cleveland; or with Mr. Chesnutt or with Mr. Davis? They could have accomplished everything that they wanted to accomplish in this great and generous city and at the same time avoided affronting and discrediting a brave and struggling group.

How different it is in other institutions and in those very institutions with which it is the ambition of Fisk University to be recognized as of equal standing in scholarship! The president and authorities of Harvard University made up their minds to ban the Negro and the Jew; but when protest came from the alumni and the public they did not ignore it; they even encouraged it. They listened to it and they followed it, and they gave up a public policy which was as extraordinary as it was wrong.

The whole policy of segregation as it is developed at Fisk University is a menace and a disgrace. I am told that this year the Jubilee Club gave a concert downtown. Not only was the colored audience "Jim-Crowed" and segregated but the colored teachers were separated from the white teachers and different windows were furnished where colored and white people were to buy their tickets! When Isaiah Scott, a bishop of the Methodist Episcopal Church, went innocently to the white window, he was refused service and insulted. I am told that the President of Fisk University took fifteen or twenty girls from the Glee Club, girls from some of the best Negro families in the United States, carried them downtown at night to a white men's club, took them down an alley and admitted them through the servants' entrance and had them sing in a basement to Southern white men, while these men smoked and laughed and talked. If Erastus Cravath, the first president of this institution, knew that a thing like that had happened at Fisk University he would, if it were in any way possible, rise from the grave and protest against this disgrace and sacrilege.

I have said that these things are taking place at Fisk University mainly through ignorance, mainly because the present workers of this institution do not realize what they are doing or why they should not do these things. But there is, I confess, one other reason, a reason so sinister and so unfortunate that I hesitate to mention it; it is this: For a long time a powerful section of the white South has offered to give its consent and countenance to the higher training of Negroes only on condition that the white South control and guide that education. And it is possible that for a million dollars the authorities of Fisk University have been asked either openly or by implication to sell to the white South the control of this institution. It is not the first time that a Corrupt Bargain of this kind has been attempted. Its earlier form at Hampton and Tuskegee included an understanding that these institutions were not to do college work and that they were to furnish servants for white people.

Sincere and long continued attempts were made to carry out this program and they failed. Hampton has become a college and is increasing its college curriculum. The graduates of Tuskegee are not servants for white people and never will be. They are entering college and the professions in larger and larger numbers. Now comes the suspicion of a similar attempt at Fisk. Pressure has been put upon Fisk graduates to go into Southern domestic service, that branch of human activity which is, as the world knows, the chief source of prostitution and the degradation of human independence. If any such bargain as I have outlined has been consciously or unconsciously, openly or secretly entered into by Fisk University, I would rather see every stone of its buildings leveled and every bit of its activity stopped before the Negro race consents.

Back, of course, of suggestions and bargains like this lies the doctrine of the inferiority of the Negro race, and I shall never believe that an institution once taught and guided by men like Cravath and Spence and Chase can ever for a moment take a stand which does not regard the black race as an equal of any other race on earth.

This brings me to the second of the two theses which I outlined, namely, that *the alumni of Fisk University are and of right ought to be the ultimate source of authority in the policy and government of this institution.* The duty of rescuing Fisk rests upon us as graduates. It is a duty we may not shirk and before which we cannot longer hesitate. I know the thing that leaps to the minds of all of us. We are aware that every great institution in this land is conducted in the last analysis by its alumni, but we echo in our own case the criticism that is so often flung at us, namely, that we have not supported this institution, that very little of this new million dollar endowment has come from us.

I resent this criticism. The students of Fisk University pay as large a proportion of their expenses as the students of Harvard or other great Northern institutions. The money which their parents have given to Fisk University and to other public purposes forms a greater proportion of their income and a more costly amount of personal sacrifice than any money that any white group has given or ever will give to this institution. It is recognized the world over today that institutions of learning are the property of the community; that the community ought to support them and that the money given for that support, either given from the public treasury or from private sources, is not a dole to beggars but a debt to society. I resent, therefore, with every ounce of my energy, the sneer that the graduates of Fisk University are beggars with no right to rule this institution simply because they are for the most part men who have struggled and toiled and done their duty for low wages and little incomes, amid mob law and prejudice:

> If blood be the price of admiralty,—
> If blood be the price of admiralty,—
> If blood be the price of admiralty,—
> Lord God, we have paid in full!

Our duty is clear before us and our right to perform that duty. The steps that we should take include, *first, Publicity.* We must let the whole world know just what is happening at Fisk University. *Secondly, Organization;* instead of the loose, ineffective Alumni Association, the alumni and friends of this institution must be firmly knit together to rescue *Alma Mater. Thirdly,* we must demand elective representation on the Board of Trustees, beginning with one or two members and gradually as the years go on increasing until in another generation we shall control the Board.

Finally, while we are taking these steps and as long as present conditions at Fisk University continue, we must actively support by our advice the boycott of this institution which has already begun. The student body at Fisk is beginning to dwindle, and the dwindling has begun with the men because the men have more economic independence than the girls. Livingston Hall houses today about one-half the number of men students which it should house. Other schools are graduating dozens of students who either began their work at Fisk University or would have been glad to go there if they could have expected to be treated as men and women. And unless that treatment is forthcoming we must not encourage colored students to go there.

I know just what this means to us of sacrifice. We love Fisk. We are its children. We believe eternally in its undying spirit; but we cannot sacrifice the ideals of the Negro race and the democracy of the world to our personal selfishness. The Negro race needs colleges. We need them today as never before; but we do not need colleges so much that we can sacrifice the manhood and womanhood of our children to the Thoughtlessness of the North or the Prejudice of the South. Ultimately Fisk will and must survive. The spirit of its great founders will renew itself, and it is that Spirit alone, reborn, which calls us tonight.

> Oh, be swift my soul, to answer Him, be jubilant my feet!
> Our God is marching on!

ENVOY

The result of that speech was an upheaval. The students danced and celebrated in exuberant glee. My daughter even feared that she might be deprived of her degree. The leading colored citizen of Nashville threatened me with personal violence if I returned. The board of trustees was angry. The President of the university was outraged and many of the alumni thought I had done a cruel and unnecessary thing. One of them wrote me, "you may be right but you'll never succeed in ousting the President." Another, a woman, took the floor after my speech and raged for fifteen minutes.

I realized that the uplift which one gets in doing what seems to be an unquestioned duty, cannot altogether compensate for its cost in friendships, in motives impugned, in lives disturbed. I went away sorry for the little president. I had no personal animus against him, but he was angry and stubborn and determined to stick to his program and fight the battle to the bitter end. He would have no elective alumni representation upon the Board of Trustees. He insisted that unless we followed his program of yielding to the South, Fisk would not get the endowment which he had started to raise.

I organized the New York Alumni and began to republish the suppressed Fisk Herald. *I published my speech and a series of unanswerable documents with signed testimony. Paul Cravath, chairman of the Board, stubbornly stood by McKenzie and the President, encouraged, instead of loosening, tightened the already severe student discipline. A year later, the students, led by George Streator, openly rebelled, and the President capped the climax by sending a half dozen of them publicly to jail. This proved the last straw. The black city rose in protest and the Trustees reluctantly sent Fayette McKenzie away.*

Education and Work

1930

Between 1910 and 1930 many changes came. Booker Washington died in 1915. The Amenia Conference [of 1916] cemented understanding between his followers and those of the National Association for the Advancement of Colored People. The Crisis *circulated widely and my word was read and listened to. It occurred to George Crawford, trained at Tuskegee, graduated at Yale, and trustee of Talladega and Howard, that this would be a fit time to crown the marriage of college and industrial education by having Howard University confer at once upon me and the president of Tuskegee an honorary degree. Mordecai Johnson, president of Howard, gladly assented and so for a moment on the campus of Howard, above the capitol of the United States, I stood upon the mountains and looked down upon my life and the life of a thousand students and reviewed that controversy whose thread had so colored and patterned my educational thought. With the blue and white hood of Howard upon my shoulders I spoke these words:*

Between the time that I was graduated from college and the day of my first experience at earning a living, there was arising in this land, and more especially within the Negro group, a controversy concerning the type of education which American Negroes needed. You, who are graduating today, have heard but echoes of this controversy and more or less vague theories of its meaning and its outcome. Perhaps it has been explained away to you and interpreted as mere misunderstanding and personal bias. If so, the day of calm review and inquiry is at hand. And I suppose that, of persons living, few can realize better than I just what that controversy meant and what the outcome is. I want then today in the short time allotted me, to state, as plainly as I may, the problem of college and industrial education for American Negroes, as it arose in the past; and then to restate it as it appears to me in its present aspect.

First of all, let me insist that the former controversy was no mere misunderstanding; there was real difference of opinion, rooted in deep sincerity on every side and fought out with a tenacity and depth of feeling due to its great importance and fateful meaning.

It was, in its larger aspects, a problem such as in all ages human beings of all races and nations have faced; but it was new in 1895 as all time is new; it was concentered and made vivid and present because of the immediate and pressing question of the education of a vast group of the children of former slaves. It was the ever new and age-young problem of Youth, for there had arisen in the South a Joseph which knew not Pharaoh—a black man who was not born in slavery. What was he to become? Whither was his face set? How should he be trained and educated? His fathers were slaves, for the most part, ignorant and poverty-stricken, emancipated in the main without land, tools, nor capital—the sport of war, the despair of economists, the grave perplexity of Science. Their children had been born in the midst of controversy, of internecine hatred, and in all the economic dislocation that follows war and civil war. In a peculiar way and under circumstances seldom duplicated, the whole program of popular education became epitomized in the case of these young black folk.

Before men thought or greatly cared, in the midst of the very blood and dust of battle, an educational system for the freedmen had been begun; and with a logic that seemed, at first, natural. The night school for adults had become the day school for children. The Negro day school had called for normal teaching and the small New England college had been transplanted and perched on hill and river in Raleigh and Atlanta, Nashville and New Orleans, and a half dozen other towns. This new Negro college was conceived of as the very foundation stone of Negro training.

But, meantime, any formal education for slaves or the children of slaves not only awakened widespread and deep-seated doubt, fear and hostility in the South but it posed, for statesmen and thinkers, the whole question as to what the education of Negroes was really aiming at, and indeed, what was the aim of educating any working class. If it was doubtful as to how far the social and economic classes of any modern state could be essentially transformed and changed by popular education, how much more tremendous was the problem of educating a race whose ability to assimilate modern training was in grave question and whose place in the nation and the world, even granted they could be educated, was a matter of baffling social philosophy? Was the nation making an effort to parallel white civilization in the South with a black civilization? Or was it trying to displace the dominant white master class with new black masters or was it seeking the difficult but surely more reasonable and practical effort of furnishing a trained set of free black laborers who might carry on in place of the violently disrupted slave system? Surely, most men said, this economic and industrial problem of the New South was the first—the central, the insistent—problem of the day.

There can be no doubt of the real dilemma that thus faced the nation, the Northern philanthropist and the black man. The argument for the New England college, which at first seemed to need no apology, grew and developed. The matter of man's earning a living, said the college, is and must be important, but surely it can never be so important as the man himself. Thus the economic adaptation of the Negro to the South must in education be subordinated to the great necessity of teaching life and culture. The South, and more especially the Negro, needed and must have trained and educated leadership if civilization was to survive. More than most, here was land and people who needed to learn the meaning of life. They needed the preparation of gifted persons for the profession of teaching, and for other professions which would in time grow. The object of education was not to make men carpenters but to make carpenters men.

On the other hand, those practical men who looked at the South after the war said: this is an industrial and business age. We are on the threshold of an economic expansion such as the world never saw before. Whatever human civilization has been or may become, today it is industry. The South because of slavery has lagged behind the world. It must catch up. Its prime necessity after the hate and holocaust of war is a trained reliable laboring class. Assume if you will that Negroes are men with every human capacity, nevertheless, as a flat fact, no rising group of peasants can begin at the top. If poverty and starvation are to be warded off, the children of the freedmen must not be taught to despise the humble work, which the mass of the Negro race must for untold years pursue. The transition period between slavery and freedom is a dangerous and critical one. Fill the heads of these children with Latin and Greek and highfalutin' notions of rights and political power, and hell will be to pay.

On the other hand, in the South, here is land and fertile land, in vast quantities, to be had at nominal prices. Here are employers who must have skilled and faithful labor, and have it now. There is in the near future an industrial development coming which will bring the South abreast with the new economic development of the nation and the world. Freedom must accelerate this development which slavery so long retarded. Here then is no time for a philosophy of economic or class revolution and race hatred. There must be friendship and good will between employer and employee, between black and white. They have common interests, and the matter of their future relations in politics and society, can well be left for the future generations and different times to solve. "Cast down your buckets where you are," cried Booker T. Washington, "in all things that are purely social we can be as separate as the fingers, yet one hand in all things essential to mutual progress."

What was needed, then, was that the Negro first should be made the intelligent laborer, the trained farmer, the skilled artisan of the South. Once he had accomplished this step in the economic world and the ladder was set for his climbing, his future would be assured, and assured on an economic foundation which would be immovable. All else in his development, if he proved himself capable of development, even to the highest, would inevitably follow. Let us have, therefore, not colleges but schools to teach the technique of industry and to make men learn by doing.

These were the opposing arguments. They were real arguments. They were set forth by earnest men, white and black, philanthropist and teacher, statesman and seer. The controversy waxed bitter. The disputants came to rival organizations, to severe social pressure, to anger and even to blows. Newspapers were aligned for and against; employment and promotion depended often on a Negro's attitude toward industrial education. The Negro race and their friends were split in twain by the intensity of their feeling and men were labelled and earmarked by their allegiance to one school of thought or to the other.

Today, all this is past; by the majority of the older of my hearers, it is practically forgotten. By the younger, it appears merely as a vague legend. Thirty-five years, a full generation and more, have elapsed. The increase in Negro education by all measurements has been a little less than marvelous. In 1895, there were not more than 1,000 Negro students of full college grade in the United States. Today, there are over 19,000 in college and nearly 150,000 in high schools. In 1895, sixty percent of American Negroes, ten years of age or over, were illiterate. Today, perhaps three-fourths can read and write. The increase of Negro students in industrial and land-grant colleges has been equally large. The latter have over 16,000 students and the increasing support of the government of the states; while the great industrial schools, especially Hampton and Tuskegee, are the best endowed institutions for the education of black folk in the world.

What then has become of this controversy as to college and industrial education for Negroes? Has it been duly settled, and if it has, how has it been settled? Has it been transmuted into a new program, and if so, what is that program? In other words, what is the present norm of Negro education, represented at once by Howard University, Fisk, and Atlanta on one hand, and by Hampton Institute, Tuskegee, and the land-grant colleges on the other?

I answer once for all, the problem has not been settled. The questions raised in those days of controversy still stand in all their validity and all their pressing insistence on an answer. They have not been answered. They must be answered, and the men and women of this audience and like audiences throughout the land are the ones from whom the world demands final reply. Answers have been offered; and the present status of the problem has enormously changed, for human problems never stand still. But I must insist that the fundamental problem is still here.

Let us see. The Negro college has done a great work. It has given us leadership and intelligent leadership. Doubtless, without these colleges the American Negro would scarcely have attained his present position. The chief thing that distinguishes the American Negro group from the Negro groups in the West Indies, and in South America, and the mother group in Africa, is the number of men that we have trained in modern education, able to cope with the white world on its own ground and in its own thought, method, and language.

On the other hand, there cannot be the slightest doubt but that the Negro college, its teachers, students, and graduates, have not yet comprehended the age in which they live: the tremendous organization of industry, commerce, capital, and credit which today forms a superorganization dominating and ruling the universe, subordinating to its ends government, democracy, religion, education, and social philosophy; and for the purpose of forcing into the places of power in this organization American black men either to guide or help reform it, either to increase its efficiency or make it a machine to improve our well-being, rather than the merciless mechanism which enslaves us; for this the Negro college has today neither program nor intelligent comprehension.

On the contrary there is no doubt but that college and university training among us has had largely the exact effect that was predicted; it has turned an increasing number of our people not simply away from manual labor and industry, not simply away from business and economic reform, into a few well-paid professions, but it has turned our attention from any disposition to study or solve our economic problem. A disproportionate number of our college-trained students are crowding into teaching and medicine and beginning to swarm into other professions and to form at the threshold of these better-paid jobs, a white-collar proletariat, depending for their support on an economic foundation which does not yet exist.

Moreover, and perhaps for this very reason, the ideals of colored college-bred men have not in the last thirty years been raised an iota. Rather in the main, they have been lowered. The average Negro undergraduate has swallowed hook, line, and sinker, the dead bait of the white undergraduate, who, born in an industrial machine, does not have to think, and does not think. Our college man today is, on the average, a man untouched by real culture. He deliberately surrenders to selfish and even silly ideals, swarming into semiprofessional athletics and Greek letter societies, and affecting to despise scholarship and the hard grind of study and research. The greatest meetings of the Negro college year like those of the white college year have become vulgar exhibitions of liquor, extravagance, and fur coats. We have in our colleges a growing mass of stupidity and indifference.

I am not counselling perfection; as desperately human groups, we must expect our share of mediocrity. But as hitherto a thick and thin defender of the college, it seems to me that we are getting into our Negro colleges considerably more than our share of plain fools.

Acquiring as we do in college no guidance to a broad economic comprehension and a sure industrial foundation, and simultaneously a tendency to live beyond our means, and spend for show, we are graduating young men and women with an intense and overwhelming appetite for wealth and no reasonable way of gratifying it, no philosophy for counteracting it.

Trained more and more to enjoy sexual freedom as undergraduates, we refuse as graduates to found and support even moderate families, because we cannot afford them; and we are beginning to sneer at group organization and race leadership as mere futile gestures.

Why is this? What is wrong with our colleges? The method of the modern college has been proven by a hundred centuries of human experience: the imparting of knowledge by the old to the young; the instilling of the conclusions of experience, "line upon line, and precept upon precept." But, of course, with this general and theoretical method must go a definite and detailed object suited to the present age, the present group, the present set of problems. It is not then in its method but in its practical objects that the Negro college has failed. It is handing on knowledge and experience but what knowledge and for what end? Are we to stick to the old habit of wasting time on Latin, Greek, Hebrew, and eschatology, or are we to remember that, after all, the object of the Negro college is to place in American life a trained black man who can do what the world today wants done; who can help the world know what it ought to want done and thus by doing the world's work well may invent better work for a better world? This brings us right back to the object of the industrial school.

Negro industrial training in the United States has accomplishments of which it has a right to be proud; but it too has not solved its problem. Its main accomplishment has been an indirect matter of psychology. It has helped bridge the transition period between Negro slavery and freedom. It has taught thousands of white people in the South to accept Negro education, not simply as a necessary evil, but as a possible social good. It has brought state support to a dozen higher institutions of learning, and to some extent, to a system of public schools. On the other hand, it has tempered and rationalized the inner emancipation of American Negroes. It made the Negro patient when impatience would have killed him. If it has not made working with the hands popular, it has at least removed from it much of the stigma of social degradation. It has made many

Negroes seek the friendship of their white fellow citizens, even at the cost of insult and caste. And thus through a wide strip of our country it has brought peace and not a sword.

But this has all been its indirect by-product, rather than its direct teaching. In its direct teaching, the kind of success which it has achieved differs from the success of the college. In the case of the industrial school, the practical object was absolutely right and still is right: that is, the desire of placing in American life a trained black man who could earn a decent living and make that living the foundation stone of his own culture and of the civilization of his group. This was the avowed object of the industrial school. How much has it done toward this? It has established some skilled farmers and among the mass some better farming methods. It has trained and placed some skilled artisans; it has given great impetus to the domestic arts and household economy; it has encouraged Negro business enterprise.

And yet we have but to remember these matters to make it patent to all that the results have been pitifully small compared with the need. Our Negro farm population is decreasing; our Negro artisans are not gaining proportionately in industry, and Negro business faces today a baffling crisis. Our success in household arts is due not to our effective teaching so much as to the medieval minds of our women who have not yet entered the machine age. Most of them seem still to think that washing clothes, scrubbing steps and paring potatoes were among the Ten Commandments.

Why now has the industrial school with all its partial success, failed absolutely in its main object when that object of training Negroes for remunerative occupation is more imperative today than thirty-five years ago?

The reason is clear: if the college has failed it is because with the right general method it has lacked definite objects appropriate to the age and race, the industrial school has failed because with a definite object it lacked appropriate method to gain it. In other words, the lack of success of the industrial education of Negroes has come not because of the absence of desperate and devoted effort, but because of changes in the world which the industrial school did not foresee, and which, even if it had foreseen, it could not have prevented, and to which it had not the ability to adapt itself.

It is easy to illustrate this. The industrial school assumed that the technique of industry in 1895, even if not absolutely fixed and permanent, was at least permanent enough for training children into its pursuit and for use as a basis of broader education. Therefore, school work for farming, carpentry, brick-laying, plastering, and painting, metal work and blacksmithing, shoemaking, sewing, and cooking was introduced and taught. But, meantime, what has happened to these vocations and trades? Machines and new industrial organizations have re-made the economic world and ousted these trades either from their old technique or their economic significance. The planing mill does today much of the work of the carpenter and the carpenter is being reduced rapidly to the level of a mere laborer. The building trades are undergoing all kinds of reconstruction, from the machine-made steel skyscraper, to the cement house cast in molds and the mass-made mail-order bungalow. Painting and masonry still survive, but the machine is after them; while printing and sewing are done by elaborate machines. Metal is being shaped by stamping mills. Nothing of shoemaking is left for the hands save mending, and in most cases, it is cheaper to buy a new shoe than to have an old one cobbled.

When it comes to the farm, a world-wide combination of circumstances is driving the farmer to the wall. Expensive machinery demands increasingly larger capital; excessive taxation of growing land values is eliminating the small owner; monopolized and manipulated markets and carriers make profits of the individual farmer small or nil; and the foreign competition of farms worked by serfs at starvation wages and backed by world-wide aggregations of capital—all this is driving farmers, black and white, from the soil and making the problem of their future existence one of the great problems of the modern world.

The industrial school, therefore, found itself in the peculiar position of teaching a technique of industry in certain lines just at the time when that technique was changing into something different, and when the new technique was a matter which the Negro school could not teach. In fact, with the costly machine, with mass production and organized distribution, the teaching of technique becomes increasingly difficult. Any person of average intelligence can take part in the making of a modern automobile, and he is paid, not for his technical training, but for his endurance and steady application.

There were many lines of factory work, like the spinning and weaving of cotton and wool, which the Negro could have successfully been set to learning, but they involved vast expenditures of capital which no school could control, and organized business at that time decreed that only white folk could work in factories. And that decree still stands. New branches of industry, new techniques are continually opening—like automobile repairing, electrical installation, and engineering—but these call for changing curricula and adjustments puzzling for a school and a set course of study,

In the attempt to put the Negro into business, so that from the inner seats of power by means of capital and credit he could control industry, we have fallen between two stools, this work being apparently neither the program of the college nor of the industrial school. The college treated it with the most approved academic detachment, while the industrial school fatuously assumed as permanent, a business organization which began to change with the nineteenth century, and bids fair to disappear with the twentieth. In 1895 we were preaching individual thrift and saving; the small retail store and the partnership for business and the conduct of industry. Today, we are faced by great aggregations of capital and world-wide credit, which monopolize raw material, carriage and manufacture, distribute their products through cartels, mergers, and chain stores, and are in process of eliminating the individual trader, the small manufacturer, and the little job. In this new organization of business the colored man meets two difficulties: first, he is not trained to take part in it; and, secondly, if he gets training, he finds it almost impossible to gain a foothold. Schools cannot teach as an art and trade that which is a philosophy, a government of men, an organization of civilization. They can impart a mass of knowledge about it, but this is the duty of the college of liberal arts and not the shop work of the trade school.

Thus the industrial school increasingly faces a blank wall and its astonishing answer today to the puzzle is slowly but surely to transform the industrial school into a college. The most revolutionary development in Negro education for a quarter-century is illustrated by the fact that Hampton today is one of the largest of Negro colleges and that her trade teaching seems bound to disappear within a few years. Tuskegee is a high school and college, with an unsolved program of the future of its trade schools. And the land-grant colleges, built to foster agriculture and industry, are becoming just like other colleges. And all this, as I said, is not the fault of the industrial school; it comes from this tremendous transformation of business, capital, and industry in the twentieth century, which few men clearly foresaw and which only a minority of men or of teachers of men today fully comprehend.

In one respect, however, the Negro industrial school was seriously at fault. It set its face toward the employer and the capitalist and the man of wealth. It looked upon the worker as one to be adapted to the demands of those who conducted industry. Both in its general program and in its classroom, it neglected almost entirely the modern labor movement. It had little or nothing to teach concerning the rise of trade unions, their present condition, and their future development. It had no conception of any future democracy in industry. That is, the very vehicle which was to train Negroes for modern industry neglected in its teaching the most important part of modern industrial development: namely, the relation of the worker to modern industry and to the modern state.

The reason for this neglect is clear. The Negro industrial school was the gift of capital and wealth. Organized labor was [long] the enemy of the black man in skilled industry. Organized labor in the United States was and [to some extent still][1]

1. Words bracketed by the editor were not in the original.

is the chief obstacle to keep black folk from earning a living by its determined policy of excluding them from unions just as long as possible and compelling them to become "scabs" in order to live. The political power of Southern white labor disfranchised Negroes, and helped build a caste system. How was the Negro industrial school easily to recognize, in this Devil of its present degradation, the Angel of its future enlightenment? How natural it was to look to white Capital and not to Labor for the emancipation of the black world—how natural and yet how insanely futile!

Here then are the successes and the failures of both Negro college and industrial school and we can clearly see that the problem still stands unsolved: How are we going to place the black American on a sure foundation in the modern state? The modern state is primarily business and industry. Its industrial problems must be settled before its cultural problems can really and successfully be attacked. The world must eat before it can think. The Negro has not found a solid foundation in that state as yet. He is mainly the unskilled laborer; the casual employee; the man hired last and fired first; the man who must subsist upon the lowest wage and consequently share an undue burden of poverty, crime, insanity, and ignorance. The only alleviation of his economic position has come from what little the industrial school could teach during the revolution of technique and from what the college took up as part of its mission in vocational training for professions.

For the college had to become a trainer of men for vocations. This is as true of the white college as of the colored college. They both tended to change their college curricula into prevocational preparation for a professional career. But the effort of the Negro college here was half-hearted. There persisted the feeling that the college had finished its work when it placed a man of culture in the world, despite the fact that our graduates who are men of culture are exceptional, and if placed in the world without ability to earn a living, what little culture they have does not long survive.

Thus, at the end of the first third of the twentieth century, while both college and industrial school can point to something accomplished, neither has reached its main objective, and they are in process of uniting to become one stream of Negro education with their great problem of object and method unsolved. The industrial school has done but little to impart the higher technique of the industrial process or of the business organization and it has done almost nothing toward putting the Negro working man in touch with the great labor movement of the white world.

On the other hand, the Negro college has not succeeded in establishing that great and guiding ideal of group development and leadership, within a dominating and expanding culture, or in establishing the cultural life as the leading motif of the educated Negro. Its vocational work has been confined to the so-called learned professions, with only a scant beginning of the imparting of the higher technique of industry and science.

The result which I have outlined is not wholly unexpected. Perhaps we can now say that it was impossible fully to avoid this situation. We have a right to congratulate ourselves that we have come to a place of such stability and such intelligence as now to be ready to grapple with our economic problem. The fact of the matter is, we have up to this time been swept on and into the great maelstrom of the white civilization surrounding us. We have been inevitably made part of that vast modern organization of life where social and political control rests in the hands of those few white folk who control wealth, determine credit, and divide income. We are in a system of culture where disparity of income is such that respect for labor as labor cannot endure; where the emphasis and outlook is not what a man does but what he is able to get for doing it; where wealth despises work and the object of wealth is to escape work, and where the ideal is power without toil.

So long as a lawyer can look forward to an income of $100,-000 a year while a maid servant is well-paid with $1,000, just so long the lawyer is going to be one hundred times more respectable than the servant and the servant is going to be called by her first name. So long as the determination of a person's income is not only beyond democratic control and public knowledge, but is a matter of autocratic power and secret manipulation, just so long the application of logic and ethics to wealth, industry and income is going to be a difficult if not insoluble problem.

In the modern world only one country is making a frontal attack upon this problem and that is Russia. Other countries are visualizing it and considering it, making some tentative and half-hearted effort, but they have not yet attacked the system as a whole, and for the most part they declare the present system inevitable and eternal and incapable of more than minor and stinted improvement.

In the midst of such a world organization we come looking for economic stability and independence. Of course, our situation is baffling and contradictory. And it is made all the more difficult for us because we are by blood and descent and popular opinion an integral part of that vast majority of mankind which is the Victim and not the Beneficiary of present conditions; which is today working at starvation wages and on a level of brute toil and without voice in its own government or education in its ignorance, for the benefit, the enormous profit, and the dazzling luxury of the white world.

Here lies the problem and it is the problem of the combined Negro college and vocational school. Without the intellectual leadership of college-bred men, we could not hitherto have held our own in modern American civilization, but must have sunk to the place of the helpless proletariat of the West Indies and of South Africa. But, on the other hand, for what has the college saved us? It has saved us for that very economic defeat which the industrial school was established to ward off and which still stands demanding solution. The industrial school acted as bridge and buffer to lead us out of the bitterness of Reconstruction to the toleration of today. But it did not place our feet upon the sound economic foundation which makes our survival in America or in the modern world certain or probable; and the reason that it did not do this was as much the fault of the college as of the trade school. The industrial school without the college was as helpless yesterday as the college is today helpless without systematic training for modern industry.

Both college and industrial school have made extraordinary and complementary mistakes in their teaching force: the industrial school secured usually as teacher a man of affairs and technical knowledge, without culture or general knowledge. The college took too often as teacher a man of books and brains with no contact with or first-hand knowledge of real everyday life and ordinary human beings, and this was true whether he taught sociology, literature, or science. Both types of teacher failed.

What then is the unescapable task of the united college and vocational school? It is without shadow of doubt a new, broad, and widely efficient vocational guidance and education for men and women of ability, selected by the most careful tests and supported by a broad system of free scholarships. Our educational institutions must graduate to the world men fitted to take their place in real life by their knowledge, spirit, and ability to do what the world wants done. This vocational guidance must have for its object the training of men who can think clearly and function normally as physical beings; who have a knowledge of what human life on earth has been, and what it is now; and a knowledge of the constitution of the known universe. All that, and in addition to that, a training which will enable them to take some definite and intelligent part in the production of goods and in the furnishing of human services and in the democratic distribution of income so as to build civilization, encourage initiative, reward effort, and support life. Just as the Negro college course with vision, knowledge and ideal must move toward vocational training, so the industrial courses must ascend from mere hand technique to engineering and industrial planning and the application of scientific and technical knowledge to problems of work and wage.

This higher training and vocational guidance must turn out young men and women who are willing not only to do the work of the world today but to provide for the future world. Here then is the job before us. It is in a sense the same kind of duty that lies before the educated white man; but it has an essential and important difference. If we make a place for ourselves in the industrial and business world today, this will be done because of our ability to establish a self-supporting organization sufficiently independent of the white organization to insure its stability and our economic survival and eventual incorporation into world industry. Ours is the double and dynamic function of tuning in with a machine in action so as neither to wreck the machine nor be crushed or maimed by it. Many think this is impossible. But if it is impossible, our future economic survival is impossible.

Let there be no misunderstanding about this, no easy going optimism. We are not going to share modern civilization just by deserving recognition. We are going to force ourselves in by organized far-seeing effort—by outthinking and outflanking the owners of the world today who are too drunk with their own arrogance and power successfully to oppose us, if we think and learn and do.

It is not the province of this paper to tell in detail just how this problem will be settled. Indeed, I could not tell you if I would. I merely stress the problem and emphasize the possibility of the solution. A generation ago, those who doubted our survival said that no alien and separate nation could hope to survive within another nation; that we must be absorbed or perish. Times have changed. Today it is rapidly becoming true that only within some great and all inclusive empire or league, can separate nations and groups find freedom and protection and economic scope for development. The small separate nation is becoming increasingly impossible and the League of Nations as well as Briand's proposed League of Europe shout this from the housetops. And just as loudly, the inevitable disintegration of the British Empire shows the impossibility of world-embracing centralized autocracy. This means that the possibility of our development and survival is clear, but clear only as brains and devotion and skilled knowledge point the way.

We need then, first, training as human beings in general

knowledge and experience; then technical training to guide and do a specific part of the world's work. The broader training should be the heritage and due of all but today it is curtailed by poverty. The technical training of men must be directed by vocational guidance which finds fitness and ability. Then actual and detailed technical training will be done by a combination of school, laboratory, and apprenticeship, according to the nature of the work and the changing technique.

The teachers of such a stream of students must be of high order. College teachers cannot follow the medieval tradition of detached withdrawal from the world. The professor of mathematics in a college has to be more than a counting machine, or proctor of examinations; he must be a living man, acquainted with real human beings, and alive to the relation of his branch of knowledge to the technical problem of living and earning a living. The teacher in a Negro college has got to be something far more than a master of a branch of human knowledge. He has got to be able to impart his knowledge to human beings whose place in the world is today precarious and critical; and the possibilities and advancement of that human being in the world where he is to live and earn a living is of just as much importance in the teaching process as the content of the knowledge taught.

The man who teaches blacksmithing must be more than a blacksmith. He must be a man of education and culture acquainted with the whole present technique and business organization of the modern world, and acquainted too with human beings and their possibilities. Such a man is difficult to procure. Because industrial schools did not have in the past such teachers for their classes and could not get them, their whole program suffered unmerited criticism. The teachers, then, cannot be pedants or dilettantes; they cannot be mere technicians and higher artisans; they have got to be social statesmen and statesmen of high order. The student body of such schools has got to be selected for something more than numbers. We must eliminate those who are here because their parents wish to be rid of them, or for the social prestige, or for passing the time, or for getting as quickly as possible into a position to make money to throw away; and we must concentrate upon young men and women of ability and vision and will.

Today there is but one rivalry between culture and vocation, college training and trade and professional training, and that is the rivalry of Time. Some day every human being will have college training. Today some must stop with the grades, and some with high school, and only a few reach college. It is of the utmost importance, then, and the essential condition of our survival and advance that those chosen for college be our best and not simply our richest or most idle.

But even this growth must be led; it must be guided by Ideals. We have lost something, brothers, wandering in strange lands. We have lost our ideals. We have come to a generation which seeks advance without ideals—discovery without stars. It cannot be done. Certain great landmarks and guiding facts must stand eternally before us; and at the risk of moralizing, I must end by emphasizing this matter of the ideals of Negro students and graduates.

The ideal of *Poverty*. This is the direct antithesis of the present American ideal of Wealth. We cannot all be wealthy. We should not all be wealthy. In an ideal industrial organization, no person should have an income which he does not personally need; nor wield a power solely for his own whim. If civilization is to turn out millionaires, it will also turn out beggars and prostitutes, either at home or among the lesser breeds without the law. A simple healthy life on limited income is the only responsible ideal of civilized folk.

The ideal of *Work*—not idleness, not dawdling, but hard continuous effort at something worth doing, by a man supremely interested in doing it, who knows how it ought to be done and is willing to take infinite pains doing it.

The ideal of *Knowledge*—not guesswork, not mere careless theory; not inherited religious dogma clung to because of fear and inertia and in spite of logic, but critically tested and laboriously gathered fact marshalled under scientific law and feeding rather than choking the glorious world of fancy and imagination, of poetry and art, of beauty and deep culture.

Finally and especially, the ideal of *Sacrifice*. I almost hesitate to mention this—so much sentimental twaddle has been written of it. When I say sacrifice, I mean sacrifice. I mean a real and definite surrender of personal ease and satisfaction. I embellish it with no theological fairy tales of a rewarding God or a milk and honey heaven. I am not trying to scare you into the duty of sacrifice by the fires of a mythical Hell. I am repeating the stark fact of survival of life and culture on this earth:

> Entbehren sollst du—sollst entbehren.
> [Thou shalt forego, shalt do without.]

The insistent problem of human happiness is still with us. We American Negroes are not a happy people. We feel perhaps as never before the sting and bitterness of our struggle. Our little victories won here and there serve but to reveal the shame of our continuing semislavery and social caste. We are torn asunder within our own group because of the rasping pressure of the struggle without. We are as a race not simply dissatisfied, we are embodied Dissatisfaction.

To increase abiding satisfaction for the mass of our people, and for all people, someone must sacrifice something of his own happiness. This is a duty only to those who recognize it as a duty. The larger the number ready to sacrifice, the smaller the total sacrifice necessary. No man of education and culture and training, who proposes to face his problem and solve it, can hope for entire happiness. It is silly to tell intelligent human beings: be good and you will be happy. The truth is today, be good, be decent, be honorable and self-sacrificing and you will not always be happy. You will often be desperately unhappy. You may even be crucified, dead and buried; and the third day you will be just as dead as the first. But with the death of your happiness may easily come increased happiness and satisfaction and fulfillment for other people—strangers, unborn babes, uncreated worlds. If this is not sufficient incentive, never try it —remain hogs.

The present census will show that the American Negro of the educated class and even of the middle industrial class is reproducing himself at an even slower rate than the corresponding classes of whites. To raise a small family today is a sacrifice. It is not romance and adventure. It is giving up something of life and pleasure for a future generation.

If, therefore, real sacrifice for others in your life work appeals to you, here it is. Here is the chance to build an industrial organization on a basis of logic and ethics, such as is almost wholly lacking in the modern world. It is a tremendous task, and it is the task equally and at once of Howard and Tuskegee, of Hampton and Fisk, of the college and of the industrial school. Our real schools must become centers of this vast crusade. With the faculty and the student body girding themselves for this new and greater education, the major part of the responsibility will still fall upon those who have already done their school work; and that means upon the alumni who, like you, have become graduates of an institution of learning. Unless the vision comes to you and comes quickly, of the educational and economic problem before the American Negro, that problem will not be solved. You not only enter, therefore, today the worshipful company of that vast body of men upon whom a great center of learning, with ancient ceremony and colorful trappings, has put the accolade of intellectual knighthood; but of men who have become the unselfish thinkers and planners of a group of people in whose hands lies the economic and social destiny of the darker peoples of the world, and by that token of the world itself.[2]

Finally, no one may fail to stress before any audience, or on any occasion and on any errand bent, the overshadowing and all-inclusive ideal of Beauty—"fair face of Beauty, all too fair to see"—fitness, rhythm, perfection of adaptation of ends to means. It is hard to mention this intelligently without maudlin sentiment and clouded words. May I speak then in parable?

Last night I saw the Zeppelin sailing in silver across the new moon. Brilliant, enormous, lovely, it symbolized the civilization

2. The printed version of this address as given in the *Journal of Negro Education* ends at this point.

over which it hung. It rode serene above miles of death; like a needle it threaded together clouds and seas, stars and continents. Within its womb were caged eternal and palpitating forces of the universe, and yet without quiver it faced the utter ends of space. Across the city, mute, dominant, magnificent, imponderable—it flew.

And what it did, men and women of Howard, you may do—you must do or die. The Zeppelin is neither miracle nor stroke of genius. It is unremittent toil and experiment and thought and infinite adaptation in the face of every discouragement and failure, in the face of death itself.

I thought, as I saw it flying there, of an angel flying low—an angel of steel and silk, with grim and awful human aim. I remembered the word of our own poet, great, but little known:[3]

> I thought I saw an angel flying low.
> I thought I saw the flicker of a wing
> Above the mulberry trees; but not again.
> Bethesda sleeps. . . .
>
> There was a day, I remember now,
> I beat my breast and cried, "Wash me God,
> Wash me with a wave of wind upon
> The barley; O quiet One, draw near, draw near!
> Walk upon the hills with lovely feet
> And in the waterfall stand and speak. . . ."

ENVOY

The reception of this speech was kindly. I think it helped. But the speech lacked something. It was strong in exposition and criticism, but weak and vague in remedy. I was at this time in my social thought entering a wider and broader ocean, and I did not yet see clearly whither I was sailing. For that illumination I have yet to wait. Perhaps my audience sensed this.

3. Du Bois is quoting from Arna Bontemps' "Nocturne at Bethesda" which won first prize in the *Crisis* poetry contest in 1926; it was first published in that magazine, December 1926; 33:66.

The Field and Function of the Negro College

1933

At Fisk University a new president had come to power.
The General Education Board had promised sorely
needed money. A new regime and a new spirit were
being built up. I myself was shortly to return to the
academic world and take up again the teaching of
sociology at the rebuilt Atlanta University. It seemed
appropriate therefore, on the occasion of my forty-fifth
anniversary of graduation, to utter a word of guidance.
I think the authorities of Fisk would have preferred my
silence. I had been in the past rather prodigal with
advice, and the results had been almost disastrous.
President [Thomas E.] Jones exhibited a little
nervousness as he extended the invitation; but I
explained to him frankly that I had no desire to prolong
my hectic career of Fisk kingmaker. I was satisfied, in
the main, with his administration, but I wanted to guide
in general the Negro college. I sensed a natural
difficulty. When the Southern Negro college changed
from a missionary school to a secular college, there was
a tendency continually to say: this college is not a
Negro college; it is a college; we are not teaching Negro
science nor Negro art; we are teaching Art and Science.
To this I wanted to oppose a word of warning. I wanted
to say in all kindness and cooperation: you are and
should and must remain a Negro college; but that
involves no low ideals.

Once upon a time some four thousand miles east of this
place, I saw the functioning of a perfect system of education. It
was in West Africa, beside a broad river; and beneath the
palms, bronze girls were dancing before the President of Liberia

and the native chiefs, to celebrate the end of the Bush Retreat and their arrival at marriageable age.

There under the Yorubas and other Sudanese and Bantu tribes, the education of the child began almost before it could walk. It went about with mother and father in their daily tasks; it learned the art of sowing and reaping and hunting; it absorbed the wisdom and folklore of the tribe; it knew the lay of land and river. Then at the age of puberty it went into the bush and there for a season the boys were taught the secrets of sex and the girls in another school learned of motherhood and marriage. They came out of the bush with a ceremony of graduation, and immediately were given and taken in marriage.

Even after that, their education went on. They sat in council with their elders and learned the history and science and art of the tribe, and practiced all in their daily life. Thus education was completely integrated with life. There could be no uneducated people. There could be no education that was not at once for use in earning a living and for use in living a life. Out of this education and out of the life it typified came, as perfect expressions, song and dance and saga, ethics and religion.

Nothing more perfect has been invented than this system of training youth among primitive African tribes. And one sees it in the beautiful courtesy of black children; in the modesty and frankness of womanhood, and in the dignity and courage of manhood; and too, in African music and art with its world-wide influence.

If a group has a stable culture which moves, if we could so conceive it, on one general level, here would be the ideal of our school and university. But, of course, this can never be achieved by human beings on any wide stage.

First and most disconcerting, men progress, which means that they change their home, their work, their division of wealth, their philosophy. And how shall men teach children that which they themselves do not know, or transmit a philosophy or religion that is already partly disbelieved and partly untrue? This is a primal and baffling problem of education and we have never wholly solved it. Or in other words, education of youth in a changing world is a puzzling problem with every temptation for lying and propaganda. But this is but the beginning of trouble. Within the group and nation significant differentiations and dislocations appear, so that education of youth becomes a preparation not for one common national life but for the life of a particular class or group; and yet the tendency is to regard as real national education only the training for that group which assumes to represent the nation because of its power and privilege, and despite the fact it is usually a small numerical minority in the nation. Manifestly in such case if a member of one of the suppressed groups receives the national education in such a land, he must become a member of the privileged aristocracy or be educated for a life which he cannot follow and be compelled to live a life which he does not like or which he deeply despises.

This is the problem of education with which the world is most familiar, and it tends to two ends: it makes the mass of men dissatisfied with life and it makes the university a system of culture for the cultured.

With this kind of university, we are most familiar. It reached in our day perhaps its greatest development in England in the Victorian era. Eton and Harrow, Oxford and Cambridge, were for the education of gentlemen—those people who inherited wealth and who by contact and early training acquired a body of manners and a knowledge of life and even an accent of English which placed them among the well-bred; these were taken up and further trained for the particular sort of life which they were to live; a life which presupposed a large income, travel, cultivated society; and activity in politics, art, and imperial industry.

This type of university training has deeply impressed the world. It is foundation for a tenacious legend preserved in fiction, poetry, and essay. There are still many people who quite instinctively turn to this sort of thing when they speak of a university. And out of this ideal arose one even more exotic and apart. Instead of the university growing down and seeking to comprehend in its curriculum the life and experience, the thought and expression of lower classes, it almost invariably tended to grow up and narrow itself to a sublimated élite of mankind.

It conceived of culture, exquisite and fragile, as a thing in itself, disembodied from flesh and action; and this culture as existing for its own sake. It was a sort of earthly heaven into which the elect of wealth and privilege and courtly address, with a few chance neophytes from the common run of men, entered and lived in a region above and apart. One gets from this that ideal of cloistered ease for Science and Beauty, partaken of by those who sit far from the noise and fury, clamor and dust of the world, as the world's aristocrats, artists and scholars.

And yet, the argument against such an ideal of a university is more an argument of fact than logic. For just as soon as such a system of training is established or as men seek to establish it, it dies. It dies like a plant without root, withering into fantastic forms, that bring ridicule or hate. Or it becomes so completely disassociated from the main currents of real life that men forget it and the world passes on as though it was not, and had not been. Thus the university cut off from its natural roots and from the mass of men, becomes a university of the air and does not establish and does not hold the ideal of universal culture which it sought, in its earlier days, to make its great guiding end.

How is it now that failure to reach this often, if not always, kills the university? The reasons to me seem clear. Human culture in its broadest and finest sense can never be wholly the product of the few. There is no natural aristocracy of man, either within a nation or among the races of the world, which unless fed copiously from without can build up and maintain and diversify a broad human culture. A system, therefore, of national education which tries to confine its benefits to preparing the few for the life of the few, dies of starvation. And this every aristocracy which the world has ever seen can prove a thousand times. There are two ways in which this can be remedied: the aristocracy may be recruited from the masses, still leaving the aim of education as the preparation of men for the life of this privileged class. This has been the desperate effort of England and in this way English aristocracy has kept its privilege and its wealth more successfully than any modern or ancient land. But even here, the method fails because the life of the English aristocrat is after all not the broadest and fullest life.

It is only, therefore, as the university lives up to its name and reaches down to the mass of universal men and makes the life of normal men the object of its training—it is only in this way that the marvelous talent and diversity and emotion of all mankind wells up through this method of human training and establishes a national culture and a national art. Herein lies the eternal logic of democracy.

Thus in the progress of human culture you have not simply a development that produces different classes of men, because classes may harmonize more or less, and above the peasant, the artisan and the merchant, may exist a leisured aristocracy and on this leisured class a class culture may be built, which may flourish long and wide. But the difficulty goes further than the narrowness and ultimate sterility of this plan. Dislocations come within these classes. Their relation to each other may change and break and the foundations upon which the cultured class has been built, may crumble. In this case your system of human training becomes not only a system for the supposed benefit of the privileged few, but cannot, indeed, carry out its function even for them. Its system of learning does not fit the mass of men nor the relations of its constituents to that mass.

One can see examples of this the world over. In Kenya, which used to be German East Africa, there are millions of black natives, and a few thousand white Englishmen who have seized and monopolized the best land, leaving the natives scarcely enough poor land for subsistence. By physical slavery, economic compulsion, or legal sanction, the natives work the land of the whites.

What kind of education will suit Kenya? The minority of landed aristocracy will be taught by tutors in Africa and then go to the great English schools and universities. The middle class of immigrant Indian merchants will learn to read and write and count at home or in elementary schools. The great mass of the black millions will be taught something of the art of agriculture, something of the work of artisans, perhaps some ability to read and write, although whether this should be in English or merely in the native tongue is a question. But on this foundation there can grow in Kenya no national university of education, because there are no national ideals. No culture, either African or European, can be built on any such economic foundation.

Thus the university, if it is to be firm, must hark back to the original ideal of the bush school. It must train the children of a nation for life and for making a living. And if it does that, and insofar as it does it, it becomes the perfect expression of the life and the center of the intellectual and cultural expression of its age.

I have seen in my life three expressions of such an ideal; all of them imperfect, all of them partial, and yet each tending toward a broad and singularly beautiful expression of universal education. My first sight of it was here at Fisk University in the fall of 1885 when I arrived as a boy of seventeen. The buildings were few, the cost of tuition, board, room and clothes was less than $200 a year; and the college numbered less than twenty-five. And yet the scheme of education as it existed in our minds, in the classroom, in the teaching of professors, in the attitude of students, was a thing of breadth and enthusiasm with an unusual unity of aim. We were a small group of young men and women who were going to transform the world by giving proof of our own ability, by teaching our less fortunate fellows so that they could follow the same path, by proclaiming to the world our belief in American democracy, and the place which Negroes would surely take in it. In none of these propositions did there exist in our minds any hesitation or doubt. There was no question as to employment and perfectly proper employment for graduates, for the ends which we had in view. There was no question of our remaining in school for no good or earnest student ever left.

Above all, to our unblinking gaze, the gates of the world would open—were opening. We never for a moment contemplated the possibility that seven millions of Americans who proved their physical and mental worth could be excluded from the national democracy of a common American culture. We came already bringing gifts. The song we sang was fresh from the lips that threw it round the world. We saw and heard the voices that charmed an emperor and a queen. We believed in the supreme power of the ballot in the hands of the masses to transform the world. Already the North was breaking the color line and for the South we were willing to wait.

I saw the same thing a few years later in Harvard University at the end of the nineteenth century. Harvard had broadened its earlier ideals. It was no longer simply a place where rich and learned New England gave the accolade to the social élite. It had broken its shell and stretched out to the West and to the South, to yellow students and to black. I had for the mere asking been granted a fellowship of $300—a sum so vast to my experience that I was surprised when it did not pay my first year's expenses. Men sought to make Harvard an expression of the United States, and to do this by means of leaders unshackled in thought and custom who were beating back bars of ignorance and particularism and prejudice. There were William James and Josiah Royce; Nathaniel Shaler and Charles Eliot Norton; George Santayana; Albert Bushnell Hart, and President Eliot himself. There were at least a dozen men—rebels against convention, unorthodox in religion, poor in money—who for a moment held in their hands the culture of the United States, typified it, expressed it, and pushed it a vast step forward. Harvard was not in 1888 a perfect expression of the American soul, or the place where the average American would have found adequate training for his life work. But perhaps it came nearer that high eminence than any other American institution had before or has since.

Again a few years later, I saw the University of Berlin. It represented in 1892 a definite and unified ideal. It did not comprehend at once the culture of all Germany, but I do not believe that ever in modern days and certainly not at Fisk or Harvard did a great university come so near expressing a national ideal. It was as though I had been stepping up from a little group college with a national vision to a provincial university with more than national outlook to a national institution which came near gathering to itself the thought and culture of forty million human beings. Every great professor of Germany, with few exceptions, had the life ambition to be called to a chair in the Friedrich Wilhelm's Universitaet zu Berlin. I sat beneath the voice of a man who perhaps more than any single individual embodied the German ideal and welded German youth into that great aggressive fist that literally put *Deutchland über Alles!* I remember well Heinrich von Treitschke. With swift flying words that hid a painfully stuttering tongue, he hammered into the young men who sat motionless and breathless beneath his voice, the doctrine of the inborn superiority of the German race. And out and around that university for a thousand miles, millions of people shared in its ideal teaching, and did this in spite of caste of birth and poverty, of jostling wealth, because they believed in an ultimate unity which Bismarckian state socialism promised. They sang their national songs and joined in national festivals with enthusiasm that brought tears to the onlooker. And it made you realize the ideal of a single united nation and what it could express in matchless poetry, daring science and undying music.

Yet in each of these cases, the ultimate ideal of a national, much less a universal university was a vision never wholly attained, and in the very nature of the case it could not be. Fisk had to be a Negro university because it was teaching Negroes and they were a caste with their own history and problems. Harvard was still a New England provincial institution and Berlin was sharply and determinedly German. Their common characteristic was that starting where they did and must, they aimed and moved toward universal culture.

Now with these things in mind, let us turn back to America and to the American Negro. It has been said many times that a Negro university is nothing more and nothing less than a university. Quite recently one of the great leaders of education in the United States, Abraham Flexner, said something of that sort concerning Howard University. As President of the Board of Trustees, he said he was seeking to build not a Negro university but a university.[1] And by those words he brought again before our eyes the ideal of a great institution of learning which becomes a center of universal culture. With all good will toward them that speak such words, it is the object of this paper to insist that there can be no college for Negroes which is not a Negro college and that while an American Negro university, just like a German or a Swiss university, may rightly aspire to a universal culture unhampered by limitations of race and culture, yet it must start on the earth where we sit and not in the skies whither we aspire. May I develop this thought.

In the first place, we have got to remember that here in America, in the year 1933, we have a situation which cannot be ignored. There was a time when it seemed as though we might best attack the Negro problem by ignoring its most unpleasant features. It was not and is not yet in good taste to speak generally about certain facts which characterize our situation in America. We are politically hamstrung. We have the greatest difficulty in getting suitable and remunerative work. Our education is more and more not only being confined to our own schools but to a segregated public school system far below the average of the nation with one-third of our children continuously out of school. And above all, and this we like least to mention, we suffer a social ostracism which is so deadening and discouraging that we are compelled either to lie about it or to turn our faces toward the red flag of revolution. It consists of the kind of studied and repeated and emphasized public insult which during all the long history of the world has led men to kill or be killed. And in the full face of any effort which any black man may make to escape this ostracism for himself,

1. Abraham Flexner (1867–1959) was a founder of the Institute for Advanced Study, at Princeton and its director for nine years. Simon and Schuster published his autobiography, *I Remember,* in 1939. For the report of the committee on Howard University, which he headed, see *New York Times,* March 15, 1932, p. 23.

stands this flaming sword of racial doctrine which will distract his effort and energy if it does not lead him to spiritual suicide.

We boast and have right to boast of our accomplishment between the days that I studied here and this forty-fifth anniversary of my graduation. It is a calm appraisal of fact to say that the history of modern civilization cannot surpass if it can parallel the advance of American Negroes in every essential line of culture in these years. And yet when we have said this we must have the common courage honestly to admit that every step we have made forward has been greeted by a step backward on the part of the American public in caste intoleration, mob law, and racial hatred.

I need but remind you that when I graduated from Fisk there was no "Jim Crow" car in Tennessee and I saw Hunter of '89 once sweep a brakeman aside at the Union Station and escort a crowd of Fisk students into the first-class seats for which they had paid. There was no legal disfranchisement and a black Fiskite sat in the legislature; and while the Chancellor of Vanderbilt University had annually to be reintroduced to the President of Fisk, yet no white Southern group presumed to dictate the internal social life of this institution.

Manifestly with all that can be said, pro and con, and in extenuation, and by way of excuse and hope, this is the situation and we know it. There is no human way by which these facts can be ignored. We cannot do our daily work, sing a song, or write a book or carry on a university and act as though these things were not.

If this is true, then no matter how much we may dislike the statement, the American Negro problem is and must be the center of the Negro university. It has got to be. You are teaching Negroes. There is no use pretending that you are teaching Chinese or that you are teaching white Americans or that you are teaching citizens of the world. You are teaching American Negroes in 1933, and they are the subjects of a caste system in the Republic of the United States of America and their life problem is primarily this problem of caste.

Upon these foundations, therefore, your university must start and build. Nor is the thing so entirely unusual or unheard of as it sounds. A university in Spain is not simply a university. It is a Spanish university. It is a university located in Spain. It uses the Spanish language. It starts with Spanish history and makes conditions in Spain the starting point of its teaching. Its education is for Spaniards, not for them as they may be or ought to be, but as they are with their present problems and disadvantages and opportunities.

In other words, the Spanish university is founded and ground in Spain, just as surely as a French university is French. There are some people who have difficulty in apprehending this very clear truth. They assume, for instance, that the French university is in a singular sense universal, and is based on a comprehension and inclusion of all mankind and of their problems. But it is not, and the assumption that it is arises simply because so much of French culture has been built into universal civilization. A French university is founded in France; it uses the French language and assumes a knowledge of French history. The present problems of the French people are its major problems and it becomes universal only so far as other peoples of the world comprehend and are at one with France in its mighty and beautiful history.

In the same way, a Negro university in the United States of America begins with Negroes. It uses that variety of the English idiom which they understand; and above all, it is founded, or it should be founded on a knowledge of the history of their people in Africa and in the United States, and their present condition. Without whitewashing or translating wish into facts, it begins with that; and then it asks how shall these young men and women be trained to earn a living and live a life under the circumstances in which they find themselves or with such changing of those circumstances as time and work and determination will permit.

Is this statement of the field of a Negro university a denial of aspiration or a change from older ideals? I do not think it is, although I admit in my own mind some change of thought and modification of method.

The system of learning which bases itself upon the actual

condition of certain classes and groups of human beings is tempted to suppress a minor premise of fatal menace. It proposes that the knowledge given and the methods pursued in such institutions of learning shall be for the definite object of perpetuating present conditions or of leaving their amelioration in the hands of and at the initiative of other forces and other folk. This was the great criticism that those of us who fought for higher education of Negroes thirty years ago, brought against the industrial school.

The industrial school founded itself and rightly upon the actual situation of American Negroes and said: "What can be done to change this situation?" And its answer was: a training in technique and method such as would incorporate the disadvantaged group into the industrial organization of the country, and in that organization the leaders of the Negro had perfect faith. Since that day the industrial machine has cracked and groaned. Its technique has changed faster than any school could teach; the relations of capital and labor have increased in complication and it has become so clear that Negro poverty is not primarily caused by ignorance of technical knowledge that the industrial school has almost surrendered its program.

In opposition to that, the proponents of college training in those earlier years said: "What black men need is the broader and more universal training so that they can apply the general principles of knowledge to the particular circumstances of their condition."

Here again was indubitable truth but incomplete truth. The technical problem lay in the method of teaching this broader and more universal truth and here just as in the industrial program, we must start where we are and not where we wish to be.

As I said a few years ago at Howard University both these positions had thus something of truth and right. Because of the peculiar economic situation in our country the program of the industrial school came to grief first and has practically been given up. Starting even though we may with the actual condition of the Negro peasant and artisan, we cannot ameliorate his condition simply by learning a trade which is the transient technique of a passing era. More vision and knowledge is needed than that. But on the other hand, while the Negro college of a generation ago set down a defensible and true program of applying knowledge to facts, it unfortunately could not completely carry it out, and it did not carry it out because the one thing that the industrial philosophy gave to education, the Negro college did not take and that was *that the university education of black men in the United States must be grounded in the condition and work of those black men!*[2]

On the other hand, it would be of course idiotic to say, as the former industrial philosophy almost said, that so far as most black men are concerned, education must stop with this. No, starting with present conditions and using the facts and the knowledge of the present situation of American Negroes, the Negro university expands toward the possession and the conquest of all knowledge. It seeks from a beginning of the history of the Negro in America and in Africa to interpret all history; from a beginning of social development among Negro slaves and freedmen in America and Negro tribes and kingdoms in Africa, to interpret and understand the social development of all mankind in all ages. It seeks to reach modern science of matter and life from the surroundings and habits and aptitudes of American Negroes and thus lead up to understanding of life and matter in the universe.

And this is a different program than a similar function would be in a white university or in a Russian university or in an English university, because it starts from a different point. It is a matter of beginnings and integrations of one group which sweep instinctive knowledge and inheritance and current reactions into a universal world of science, sociology, and art. In no other way can the American Negro college function. It cannot begin with history and lead to Negro history. It cannot start with sociology and end with[3] Negro sociology.

Why was it that the Renaissance of literature which began among Negroes ten years ago has never taken real and lasting

2. Italics added by Du Bois in manuscript.
3. In the original this reads "lead to."

root? It was because it was a transplanted and exotic thing. It was a literature written for the benefit of white people and at the behest of white readers, and starting out primarily from the white point of view. It never had a real Negro constituency and it did not grow out of the inmost heart and frank experience of Negroes; on such an artificial basis no real literature can grow.

On the other hand, if starting in a great Negro university you have knowledge, beginning with the particular, and going out to universal comprehension and unhampered expression, you are going to begin to realize for the American Negro the full life which is denied him now. And then after that comes a realization of the older object of our college—to bring this universal culture down and apply it to the individual life and individual conditions of living Negroes.

The university must become not simply a center of knowledge but a center of applied knowledge and guide of action. And this is all the more necessary now since we easily see that planned action especially in economic life is going to be the watchword of civilization.

If the college does not thus root itself in the group life and afterward apply its knowledge and culture to actual living, other social organs must replace the college in this function. A strong, intelligent family life may adjust the student to higher culture; and, too, a social clan may receive the graduate and induct him into life. This has happened and is happening among a minority of privileged people. But it costs society a fatal price. It tends to hinder progress and hamper change—it makes education propaganda for things as they are. It leaves the mass of those[4] without social standing—misfits and rebels who despite their education are uneducated in its meaning and application. The only college which stands for the progress of all—mass as well as aristocracy—functions in root and blossom as well as in the overshadowing and heaven-filling tree. No system of learning—no university—can be universal before it is German, French, Negro. Grounded in inexorable fact and con-

4. In the original appear four words here omitted: "without family training and."

dition, in Poland or Italy, it may seek the universal, and haply it may find it—and finding it bring it down to earth and to us.

We have imbibed from the surrounding white world a childish idea of progress. Progress means bigger and better results always and forever. But there is no such rule of life. In six thousand years of human culture, the losses and retrogressions have been enormous. We have no assurance that twentieth-century civilization will survive. We do not know that American Negroes will survive. There are sinister signs about us, antecedent to and unconnected with the great depression. The organized might of industry north and south is relegating the Negro to the edge of survival and using him as a labor reservoir on starvation wage. No secure professional class, no science, literature, nor art can live on such a subsoil. It is an insistent deep-throated cry for rescue, guidance, and organized advance that greets the black leader today and the college that trains him has got to let him know at least as much about the great black miners' strike in Alabama as about the Age of Pericles.[5] By singular accident—almost by compelling fate—I drove by, as I came here yesterday, the region where I taught a country school over forty years ago. There is no progress there. There is only space, disillusion, and death beside the same eternal hills. There where first I heard the "Sorrow Songs" are the graves of men and women and children who had the making of a fine intelligent upstanding yeomanry. There remains but the half-starved farmer, the casual laborer, the unpaid servant. Why, in a land rich with wealth, muscle, and colleges?

To the New Englander of wealth and family, Harvard and Yale are parts and only parts of a broad training which the New England home begins and a State Street or Wall Street business ends. How fine and yet how fatal! There lie root and reason for the World War and the Great Depression. To the American Negro, culture must adjust itself to a different family history and apply itself to a new system of social caste and in

5. As reprinted in the *Crisis*, August 1933, the conclusion of this paragraph and the entirety of the next is not included.

this adjustment comes new opportunity of making education and progress possible and not antagonistic.

We are on the threshold of a new era. Let us not deceive ourselves with outworn ideals of wealth and servants and luxuries, reared on a foundation of ignorance, starvation and want. Instinctively, we have absorbed these ideals from our twisted white American environment. This new economic planning is not for us unless we do it. Unless the American Negro today, led by trained university men of broad vision, sits down to work out by economics and mathematics, by physics and chemistry, by history and sociology, exactly how and where he is to earn a living and how he is to establish a reasonable life in the United States or elsewhere, unless this is done the university has missed its field and function and the American Negro is doomed to be a suppressed and inferior caste in the United States for incalculable time.

Here, then, is a job for the American Negro university. It cannot be successfully ignored or dodged without the growing menace of disaster. I lay the problem before you as one which you must not ignore.

To carry out this plan, two things and only two things are necessary—teachers and students. Buildings and endowments may help, but they are not indispensable. It is necessary first to have teachers who comprehend this program and know how to make it live among their students. This is calling for a good deal, because it asks that teachers teach that which they have learned in no American school and which they never will learn until we have a Negro university of the sort that I am visioning. No teacher, black or white, who comes to a university like Fisk, filled simply with general ideas of human culture or general knowledge of disembodied science, is going to make a university of this school. Because a university is made of human beings, learning of the things they do not know from things they do know in their own lives.

And secondly, we must have students. They must be chosen for ability to learn. There is always the temptation to assume that the children of privileged classes, the rich, the noble, the white, are those who can best take education. One has but to express this to realize its utter futility. But perhaps the most dangerous thing among us is for us, without thought, to imitate the white world and assume that we can choose students at Fisk because of the amount of money which their parents have happened to get hold of. That basis of selection is going to give us an extraordinary aggregation. We want by the nicest methods possible, to seek out the talented and the gifted among our constituency, quite regardless of their wealth or position, and to fill this university and similar institutions with persons who have got brains enough to take fullest advantage of what the university offers. There is no other way. With teachers who know what they are teaching and whom they are teaching and the life that surrounds both the knowledge and the knower, and with students who have the capacity and the will to absorb this knowledge, we can build the sort of Negro university which will emancipate not simply the black folk of the United States, but those white folk who in their effort to suppress Negroes have killed their own culture—men who in their desperate effort to replace equality with caste and to build inordinate wealth on a foundation of abject poverty have succeeded in killing democracy, art, and religion.

Only a universal system of learning, rooted in the will and condition of the masses and blossoming from that manure up toward the stars is worth the name. Once builded it can only grow as it brings down sunlight and star shine and impregnates the mud. The chief obstacle in this rich land endowed with every natural resource and with the abilities of a hundred different peoples—the chief and only obstacle to the coming of that kingdom of economic equality which is the only logical end of work, is the determination of the white world to keep the black world poor and make themselves rich. The disaster which this selfish and short-sighted policy has brought lies at the bottom of this present depression, and too, its cure lies beside it. Your clear vision of a world without wealth, of capital without profit, of income based on work alone, is the path out not only for you but for all men.

Is not this a program of segregation, emphasis of race and particularism as against national unity and universal humanity? It is, and it is not by choice but by force; you do not get humanity by wishing it nor do you become American citizens simply because you want to. A Negro university from its high ground of unfaltering facing of the Truth, from its unblinking stare at hard facts, does not advocate segregation by race, it simply accepts the bald fact that we are segregated, apart, hammered into a separate unity by spiritual intolerance and legal sanction backed by mob law, and that this separation is growing in strength and fixation; that it is worse today than a half century ago and that no character, address, culture, or desert is going to change it, in our day or for centuries to come.

Recognizing this brute fact, groups of cultured, trained, and devoted men gathering in great institutions of learning proceed to ask: What are we going to do about it? It is silly to ignore and gloss the truth; it is idiotic to proceed as though we were white or yellow, English or Russian. Here we stand. We are American Negroes. It is beside the point to ask whether we form a real race. Biologically we are mingled of all conceivable elements, but race is psychology, not biology; and psychologically we are a unified race with one history, one red memory, and one revolt. It is not ours to argue whether we will be segregated or whether we ought to be a caste. We are segregated; we are a caste. This is our given and at present unalterable fact. Our problem is: How far and in what way can we consciously and scientifically guide our future so as to insure our physical survival, our spiritual freedom and our social growth? Either we do this or we die. There is no alternative. If America proposes the murder of this group, its moral descent into imbecility and crime and its utter loss of manhood, self-assertion, and courage, the sooner we realize this the better. By that great line of McKay: "If we must die, let it not be like hogs."

But the alternative of not dying like hogs is not that of dying or killing like snarling dogs. It is rather conquering the world by thought and brain and plan; by expression and organized cultural ideals. Therefore, let us not beat futile wings in impotent frenzy, but carefully plan and guide our segregated life, organize in industry and politics to protect it and expand it, and above all to give it unhampered spiritual expression in art and literature. It is the council of fear and cowardice to say this cannot be done. What must be can and it is only a question of Science and Sacrifice to bring the great consummation.

What that will be, none knows. It may be a great physical segregation of the world along the color line; it may be an economic rebirth which insures spiritual and group integrity amid physical diversity. It may be utter annihilation of class and race and color barriers in one ultimate mankind, differentiated by talent, susceptibility and gift—but any of these ends are matters of long centuries and not years. We live in years, swift flying, transient years. We hold the possible future in our hands but not by wish and will, only by thought, plan, knowledge, and organization. If the college can pour into the coming age an American Negro who knows himself and his plight and how to protect himself and fight race prejudice, then the world of our dream will come and not otherwise.[6]

> The golden days are gone. Why do we wait
> So long upon the marble steps, blood
> Falling from our open wounds? and why
> Do our black faces search the empty sky?
> Is there something we have forgotten?
> Some precious thing we have lost,
> Wandering in strange lands?

What we have lost is the courage of independent self-assertion. We have had as our goal—American full citizenship, nationally recognized. This has failed—flatly and decisively failed. Very well. We're not dead yet. We are not going to die. If we use our brains and strength there is no way to stop our ultimate triumph as creators of modern culture—if we use our strength and brains.

And what pray stops us but our dumb caution—our fear—our very sanity. Let us then be insane with courage.

6. As published in the *Crisis*, August 1933, the essay ends at this point. The first stanza of poetry is from Arna Bontemps's "Nocturne at Bethesda" first published in the *Crisis*, December 1926. The last eight lines may have been Du Bois's own; they have not been otherwise identified.

Like a mad man's dream, there came
One fair, swift flash to me
Of distances, of streets aflame
With joy and agony;
And further yet, a moonlit sea
Foaming across its bars
And further yet, the infinity
Of wheeling suns and stars.

ENVOY

There was no aftermath of this speech save perhaps a general satisfaction. But to me it was the beginning of a new line of thought. The argument of the Howard speech did not seem to me to be altogether final. Something was missing and from that day I began to read and study Karl Marx.[7] I began to understand my recent visit to Russia. I became interested in the New Deal and I wanted to supplement the liberalism of Charles Sumner with the new economic contribution of the twentieth century.

7. Du Bois must mean here an intensive study of Marx—and by 1934 he taught a course on "Marx and the Negro Question" at Atlanta University. But he had read in Marx much earlier and by 1904 there are indications that he thought of himself as basically a socialist. His "visit to Russia" had occurred in 1926.

The Revelation of
Saint Orgne the Damned

1938

*On the fiftieth anniversary of my graduation I spoke
again at Fisk University with kindly welcome and
expectation. Many of the professors, remembering the
rather cryptic title of my other speeches, searched the
encyclopedias for the "Saint Orgne" who appeared in the
title of my address. They did not find him. I had to
explain that it was but a familiar anagram of a well-
known word: Negro. I was here speaking a word of
benediction, not merely to the three surviving members
of my own class or to the graduating class of the day;
I was speaking to the intelligent colored citizens of 1938
and seeking to express a certain philosophy of life. I
was at the entrance of the valley of the shadow of death
and the view was splendid.*

Saint Orgne stood facing the morning and asked: What
is this life I see? Is the dark damnation of color, real? or simply
mine own imagining? Can it be true that souls wrapped in black
velvet have a destiny different from those swathed in white
satin or yellow silk, when all these coverings are fruit of the
same worm, and threaded by the same hands? Or must I, ignoring all seeming difference, rise to some upper realm where there
is no color nor race, sex, wealth nor age, but all men stand equal
in the Sun?

Thus Orgne questioned Life on his Commencement morning,
in the full springtide of his day. And this is the Revelation and
the answer that came to Saint Orgne the Damned as he came to
be called, as he stood on his Mount of Transfiguration, looking
full at life as it is and not as it might be or haply as he would
have it.

"In very truth, thou art damned, and may not escape by vain

103

imagining nor fruitless repining. When a man faces evil, he does not call it good, nor evade it; he meets it breastforward, with no whimper of regret nor fear of foe."

"Blessed is he that reads and they that hear the words of this prophecy for the time is at hand. Grace be unto you and peace, from him which was and which is and is to come and from the seven spirits which are before his throne."

I, who also am your brother and companion in tribulation and in the kingdom and the patience, was in the isle that is called America. I was in the spirit and heard behind me a great Voice saying, "I am Alpha and Omega, the first and the last; and what thou seest write." I turned to the voice. I saw seven golden candlesticks with one in the midst of the candlesticks; and in his hands seven stars and out of his mouth went a sharp two-edged sword. And when I saw him I fell at his feet as dead and he laid his right hand upon me saying unto me "Fear not. Write thou the things which thou hast seen; the mystery of the seven stars and the seven golden candlesticks."

So Orgne turned and climbed the Seven Heights of Hell to view the Seven Stars of Heaven. The seven heights are Birth and Family; School and Learning; the University and Wisdom; the great snow-capped peak of Work; the naked crag of Right and Wrong; the rolling hills of the Freedom of Art and Beauty; and at last, the plateau that is the Democracy of Race; beyond this there are no vales of Gloom—for the star above is the sun itself and all shadows fall straight before it.

Orgne descended into the valleys of the Shadow, lit only by the waving light of single candles set in seven golden candlesticks, struggling through noisome refuse of body and mind. Long years he strove, uphill and down, around and through seven groups of seven years until in the end he came back to the beginning, world-weary, but staunch; and this is the revelation of his life and thought which I, his disciple, bring you from his own hands.

A golden candlestick stood beneath a silver star, atop a high mountain and in the cold gray dawn of a northern spring. There was the first hint of apple blossoms and faint melody in the air; within the melody was the whisper of a Voice, which sighed and said: "Why should we breed black folk in this world and to what end? Wherefore should we found families and how? Is not the word for such as are born white and rich?"

Then Orgne, half grown, lying prone, reared himself suddenly to his feet and shivering looked upward to light. The sun rose slowly above the mountain and with its light spake. Hear ye the Wisdom of the families of black folk:

Gentlemen are bred and not born. They are trained in childhood and receive manners from those who surround them and not from their blood. Manners maketh Man, and are the essence of good breeding. They have to do with forms of salutation between civilized persons; with the care and cleanliness and grooming of the body. They avoid the stink of bodily excretions; they eat their food without offense to others; they know that dirt is matter misplaced and they seek to replace it. The elementary rules of health become to them second nature and their inbred courtesy one to another makes life liveable and gracious even among crowds.

Now this breeding and infinite detail of training is not learned in college and may not be taught in school. It is the duty and task of the family group and once the infinite value of that training is missed it can seldom be replaced through any later agency. It is in vain that the university seeks to cope with ill-bred youngsters, foul-mouthed loafers and unwashed persons who have happened to pass the entrance examinations. Once in the earlier mission schools among American Negroes men tried to do this, knowing of the irreparable harm slavery had done the family group. They had some success right here in this institution; but the day when such effort is possible is gone. Unless a new type of Negro family takes the burden of this duty, we are destined to be, as we are too largely today, a bad-mannered, unclean crowd of ill-bred young men and women who are under the impression that they are educated.

For this task we have got to create a new family group; and a cultural group rather than a group merely biological. The biology and blood relationship of families is entirely subordinate and unimportant as compared with its cultural entity; with the presence of two persons who take upon themselves voluntarily the sacrificial priesthood of parents to children, limited in number and interval by intelligent and scientific birth-control, who can and will train in the elements of being civilized human beings: how to eat, how to sleep, how to wash, how to stand, how to walk, how to laugh, how to be reverent and how to obey.

It is not entirely our fault that we have missed, forgotten or are even entirely unaware of the cultural place of the family. In European and American civilization we have tried to carry out the most idiotic paradox that ever civilized folk attempted. We have tried to make babies both sins and angels. We have regarded sex as a disgrace and as eternal life. We talk in one breath of the Virgin Mary and of the Mother of God. And at the critical age of life for both men and women, we compel them to strain the last sinew of moral strength to repress a natural and beautiful appetite, or to smear it with deception and crime. We base female eligibility for marriage on exotic personal beauty and childlike innocence, and yet pretend to desire brains, common sense and strength of body. If an age thus immolates its ugly virgins, it will crucify its beautiful fools, with the result of making marriage a martyrdom that few enter with open eyes. The change from this has got to recognize the sin of virginity in a world that needs proper children; the right of the so-called unfathered child to be; the legal adoption into the cultural family of gifted and promising children and the placing of black sheep, no matter who their parents are, under necessary restraint and correction. Amen.

The Voice ceased. As Orgne walked slowly down the mountain, he brooded long over the word he had heard, wondering vaguely how far the revelation was within or without his own soul; and then turning the message over in his mind, he thought of his own home, of the three small rooms, of the careful, busy mother and grandmother, of the dead father; and he mused: if one's start in life depends on breeding and not on color or unchangeable and unfathomable compulsions before births, surely I may live, even though I am black and poor.

There came a long space of seven years. Orgne stood by the

bank of the Golden River, with the second candlestick in his hand. He could not see the stars above, for it was nine o'clock of a sun-washed morning; but he knew they were there. He was celebrating all alone his entry into high school. None of his people save only his dead grandfather had ever gotten so far; but with the wave of disappointment which comes with all accomplishment, he muttered, "And why should they, why should I, dawdle here with elements of things and mere tools of Knowledge while both I and the world wait." The river flowed softly as he slept in the summer mildness. Daisies and buttercups waved above him. The grey fleecy clouds gathered and swiftly low thunder rolled; a bolt of heat lightning flashed across the sky. He slept on, yet heard the second star as it spoke:

Hear ye! This is the wisdom of the elementary school.

The difficulty and essential difficulty with Negro education lies in the elementary school; lies in the fact that the number of Negroes in the United States today who have learned thoroughly to read, write, and count is small; and that the proportion of those who cannot read, cannot express their thoughts and cannot understand the fundamentals of arithmetic, algebra and geometry is discouragingly large. The reason that we cannot do thorough college work and cannot keep high university standards is that the students in institutions like this are fundamentally weak in mastery of those essential tools to human learning. Not even the dumbest college professor can spoil the education of the man who as a child has learned to read, write, and cipher; so too Aristotle, Immanuel Kant and Mark Hopkins together are powerless before the illiterate who cannot reason.

The trouble lies primarily, of course, in the elementary schools of the South; in schools with short terms; with teachers inadequate both as to numbers and training; with quarters ill-suited physically and morally to the work in hand; with colored principals chosen not for executive ability but for their agility in avoiding race problems; and with white superintendents who try to see how large a statistical showing can be made without expenditure of funds, thought, or effort.

This is the fault of a nation which does not thoroughly believe in the education of Negroes, and of the South which still to a large extent does not believe in any training for black folk which is not of direct commercial profit to those who dominate the state.

But the fault does not end there. The fault lies with the Negroes themselves for not realizing this major problem in their education and for not being willing and eager and untiring in their effort to establish the elementary school on a fundamental basis. Necessary as are laws against lynching and race segregation, we should put more money, effort, and breath in perfecting the Negro elementary school than in anything else, and not pause nor think of pausing until every Negro child between five and fifteen is getting at least nine months a year, five hours a day, five days in the week, in a modern school room, with the best trained teachers, under principals selected for training and executive ability, and serving with their teachers during efficiency and good behavior; and with the school under the control of those whose children are educated there.

Until this is done and so far as it is not done the bulk of university endowment is being wasted and high schools strive partially in vain. Amen.

Again flew seven years. Orgne was far from home and school and land. He was speaking an unknown tongue and looking upon the walls and towers, colors and sounds of another world. It was high noon and autumn. He sat in a lofty cathedral, glorious in the fretted stone lace-work of its proudly vaulted roof. Its flying buttresses looked down upon a grey and rippled lake; beyond lay fields of flowers, golden chrysanthemums and flaming dahlias and further the ancient university, where for a thousand years men had sought Truth. Around rose a symphony of sound, a miraculous blending of strings and brass, trumpet and drum which was the Seventh Symphony with its lovely interlacing of melody and soft solemn marches, breaking to little hymns and dances. He listened to its revelation gazing rapt at candlesticks and gilded star and whispered: "Why should I know and what, and what is the end of knowing? Is it not enough to feel?" The angels in the choir sang No—Hear ye! For Wisdom is the principal thing.

There can be no iota of doubt that the chief trouble with the world and the overwhelming difficulty with American Negroes is widespread ignorance; the fact that we are not thoroughly acquainted with human history; of what men and peoples have thought and done in the seven thousand years of our cultural life. We are especially unacquainted with modern science; with the facts of matter and its constitution; with the meaning of time and space; with chemical reaction and electrical phenomena; with history of the machine and the tool; with the unfolding of life in the vegetable and animal kingdoms; with the history of human labor; the development of our knowledge of the mind; the practical use of the languages of the world; and the methods of logical reasoning, beginning and ending with mathematics.

This great body of knowledge has been growing and developing for thousands of years, and yet today its mastery is in the hands of so few men, that a comparatively small death roll would mean the end of human culture. Without this knowledge there can be no planning in economy; no substantial guidance in character building; no intelligent development of art. It is for acquaintanceship with this knowledge and the broadening of its field that the college and university exist. This is the reason and the only reason for its building among American Negroes and the work that it is accomplishing today is so infinitely less than that which with any real effort it might accomplish that one has a right to shudder at the misuse of the word university. Amen.

Orgne stood at twilight in the swamp. In seven more years, all the romance and glamour of Europe had sunk to the winter of America. It was twilight, and the swamp glowed with the mystery of sunset—long shafts of level burning light—greens and yellows, purples and red; the whisper of leaves, the ghosts of dead and dying life. The sun died dismally, and the clouds gathered and drizzling rain began to fall with slow determination. Orgne shrank within himself. He saw the toil of labor and revolted. He felt the pinch of poverty and wept. "What is this stuff I hear," he cried: "how can we marry and support a family without money? How can we control our schools without economic resource? How can we turn our churches from centers of superstition into intelligent building of character; and beyond this how shall we have time for real knowledge; and freedom of art; and effort toward world-wide democracy, until we have the opportunity to work decently and the resources to spend, which shall enable us to be civilized human beings?"

Suddenly across the swamp and across the world and up from the cotton fields of Georgia rolled a Negro folk song. Orgne saw in music Jehovah and his angels, the Wheel in a Wheel. He saw the Golden Candlestick and heard the revelation of the Star: Hear ye! This is the teaching of the World of Work.

The most distressing fact in the present world is poverty; not absolute poverty, because some folk are rich and many are well-to-do; not poverty as great as some lands and other historical ages have known; but poverty more poignant and discouraging because it comes after a dream of wealth; of riotous, wasteful and even vulgar accumulation of individual riches, which suddenly leaves the majority of mankind today without enough to eat; without proper shelter; without sufficient clothing.

Nowhere was the dream of wealth, for all who would work and save, more vivid than here in the United States. We Negroes sought to share that vision and heritage. Moreover, the poverty which the world now experiences, comes after startling realization of our national endowment of rich natural resources and our power to produce. We have the material goods and forces at command, the machines and technique sufficient to feed, clothe the world, educate children and free the human soul for creative beauty and for the truth that will widen the bounds of all freedom.

That does not mean that we could have enough goods and services for present extravagance, display and waste; but if there were neither idle rich nor idle poor; if sharing of wealth were based not on owning but only on effort, and if all who are able did their share of the world's work or starved, and limited their consumption to reasonable wants, we could abolish poverty.

Why have we not done this? It is because of greed in the production and distribution of goods and human labor. We discovered widely in the eighteenth century and the nineteenth the use of capital and it was a great and beneficent discovery; it was the rule of sacrificing present wealth for greater wealth to come. But instead of distributing this increase of wealth primarily among those who make it we left most workers as poor as possible in order further to increase the wealth of a few. We produced more wealth than the wealthy could consume and yet used this increased wealth to monopolize materials and machines; to buy and sell labor in return for monopoly ownership in the products of labor and for further wealth.

We thus not only today produce primarily for the profit of owners and not for use of the mass of people, but we have grown to think that this is the only way in which we can produce. We organize industry for private wealth and not for public weal, and we argue often honestly and conscientiously, that no human planning can change the essentials of this process: Yet the process itself has failed so many times and so abysmally, that we are bound to change or starve in the midst of plenty. We are encouraging war through fear of poverty that need not exist; we face the breakdown of production by persistent overproduction of the kinds of goods which we cannot afford to consume.

What can we do? There is only one thing for civilized human beings to do when facing such a problem, and that is to learn the facts, to reason out their connection and to plan the future; to know the truth; to arrange it logically and to contrive a better way. In some way, as all intelligent men acknowledge, we must in the end, produce for the satisfaction of human needs and distribute in accordance with human want. To contend that this cannot be done is to face the Impossible Must. The blind cry of reaction on the one hand, which says that we cannot have a planned economy and, therefore, must not try; and the cry of blood which says that only by force can selfishness be curbed, are equally wrong. It is not a question of deliberate guilt but of selfish stupidity. The economic world can only be reformed by Spartan restraint in the consumption of goods and the use of services; by the will to work not simply for individual profit but for group weal; not simply for one group but for all groups; and the freedom to dream and plan.

This reformation of the world is beginning with agony of soul and strain of muscle. It can and must go on, and we black folk of America are faced with the most difficult problem of realizing and knowing the part which we have got to play in this economic revolution for our own salvation and for the salvation of the world. This is not easy, for we are cut off from the main effort by the lesions of race; by the segregation of color; by the domination of caste. And yet nothing could be more fatal to our own ideals and the better ideals of the world than for us with unconscious ignorance or conscious perversity or momentary applause to join the forces of reaction; to talk as though the twentieth century presented the same oversimplified path of economic progress which seemed the rule in the nineteenth: work, thrift and wealth by individual effort no matter what the social cost.

The economic illiteracy prevalent among American Negroes is discouraging. In a day when every thinker sees the disorganization of our economic life and the need of radical change, we find the teachers of economics in colored colleges, the Negro business men, Negro preachers and writers to a very large extent talking the language of the early nineteenth century; seeking to make themselves believe that work for any kind of wages, saving at any sacrifice and wealth on any terms not excluding cheating, murder, and theft, are ways of the world still open and beckoning to us. Selah!

Orgne listened and sat staring at the sodden cotton field beyond the somber swamp. Always the swinging thunder of song surged above—Jordan rolled; the rocks and the mountains fled away, the Way was crowded; and Moses went down, away down among the cabins in the cotton patch to the crazy church and hysterical crowd of penitents all praying madly to escape debt. Orgne talked to the planter and said "let my people go," and worked with the tenants seven long years.

Seven years he toiled and in the end had a little nest of land holders owning one large unmortgaged farm in twenty shares; working their crops and buying their provisions in common and dividing them with equal justice. Poor, Orgne came to them and poor he finally went away leaving them poor too but fed and sheltered. They called him Saint. He smiled and looked upward to the star; but the preacher looked down to the dirt and mortgaged it behind the backs of the trusting flock and ran away with the money.

Saint Orgne cursed and cried: how shall we plan a new earth without honest men and what is this thing we call a church. So, angry, disillusioned and weary he came to a land where it was always afternoon, and he laid him prone on the earth and slept.

Seven years he slept and in seven years came a thousand miles and more to Ohio, to teach in college. At high noon he stood before the chapel and heard the singing of a hymn in the haze of early spring time. Around him stretched the wide, undulating valleys of the Miami, the Ohio, and the realm of the Mississippi. He looked up and suddenly hated the walls that shut out the stars; he hated the maudlin words of the hymn quite as much as he loved the lilt of the voices that raised it. He loved the flowers—the violets and morning glory, the blossoming fruit that filled the yards about. Then came the earthquake; then the earth trembled and swayed; far off in San Francisco a city fell and around the nation quivered. In the midst of the rushing, swaying crowd, again Orgne, after seven years, awoke and found the Golden Candlestick in his hands, and heard the low clear revelation of the Star:

Saint Orgne the Damned, behold the Vision of the Seven Black Churches of America,— the Baptist, the four wings of Methodism, the Roman and Episcopal Catholics.

Their five millions of members in 40,000 groups, holding $200,000,000 in their hands, are the most strongly organized body among us; the first source of our group culture, the beginning of our education—what is this church doing today toward its primary task of teaching men right and wrong, and the duty of doing right?

The flat answer is nothing, if not less than nothing. Like other churches and other religions of other peoples and ages, our church has veered off on every conceivable side path, which interferes with and nullifies its chief duty of character building.

It has built up a body of dogma and fairy tale, fantastic fables of sin and salvation, impossible creeds and impossible demands for ignorant unquestioning belief and obedience. Ask any thorough churchman today and he will tell you, not that the object of the church is to get men to do right and make the majority of mankind happy, but rather that the whole duty of man is to "believe in the Lord Jesus Christ and be saved;" or to believe in the "one Holy and Catholic church," infallible and omniscient; or to keep the tomb of one's grandfather intact and his ideas undisputed.

Considering how desperately great and good men have inveighed against these continuing foibles of priesthood for many thousand years, and how little in essence has been accomplished, it may seem hopeless to return to the attack today, but that is precisely what this generation has to do. The function of the Negro church, instead of being that of building edifices, paying old debts, holding revivals and staging entertainments, has got to be brought back, or shall we say forward, to the simple duty of teaching ethics. For this purpose the Hebrew scriptures and the New Testament canon will not suffice. We must stop telling children that the lying and deceitful Jacob was better than the lazy Esau, or that the plan of salvation is anything but the picture of the indecent anger and revenge of a bully.

We can do this, not so much by the attacking of outworn superstition and conventional belief as by hearty research into real ethical questions. When is it right to lie? Do low wages mean stealing? Does the prosperity of a country depend upon the number of its millionaires? Should the state kill a murderer? How much money should you give to the poor? Should there be any poor? And as long as there are, what is crime and who are the criminals?

So Saint Orgne preached the word of life from Jeremiah, Shakespeare and Jesus, Confucius, Buddha, and John Brown; and organized a church with a cooperative store in the Sunday school room; with physician, dentist, nurse and lawyer to help, serve and defend the congregation; with library, nursery school, and a regular succession of paid and trained lecturers and discussion; they had radio and moving pictures and out beyond the city a farm with house and lake. They had a credit union, group insurance and building and loan association. The members paid for this not by contributions but by ten dollars a month each of regular dues and those who would join this church must do more than profess to love God.

Seven years he served, and married a woman not for her hair and color but for her education, good manners, common sense, and health. Together they made a home and begot two strong intelligent children. Looking one day into their eyes Orgne became suddenly frightened for their future. He prayed "Oh life let them be free!"

So soon, so soon, Orgne sighed, the world rolls around its seven years. It was midsummer and he was sailing upon the sea. He was bound for Africa on a mission of world brotherhood. Behind and waiting were wife and children, home and work. Ahead was the darker world of men yellow, brown, and black. Dinner was done and the deck empty save for himself; all were within the magnificent saloon massed with tall vases of roses and lilies, priceless with tapestry and gilding, listening to the great organ which the master played. The largo whispered, smiled and swelled upward to tears. Then the storm swept down. Then the ocean, lashed to fury by the wind, bellowed and burned; the vast ship tossed like a tortured soul, groaned and twisted in its agony. But Orgne smiled. He knew that behind the storm and above the cloud the evening stars were singing, and he listened to the rhythm of their words: Hear ye! This is the Freedom of Art which is the Beauty of Life.

Life is more than meat, even though life without food dies. Living is not for earning, earning is for living. The man that spends his life earning a living, has never lived. The education that trains men simply for earning a living is not education.

What then is Life—What is it for—What is its great End? Manifestly in the light of all knowledge, and according to the testimony of all men who have lived, Life is the fullest, most complete enjoyment of the possibilities of human existence. It is the development and broadening of the feelings and emotions, through sound and color, line and form. It is technical mastery of the media that these paths and emotions need for expression of their full meaning. It is the free enjoyment of every normal appetite. It is giving rein to the creative impulse, in thought and imagination. Here roots the rise of the Joy of Living, of music, painting, drawing, sculpture and building; hence come literature with romance, poetry, and essay; hence rise Love, Friendship, emulation, and ambition, and the ever widening realms of thought, in increasing circles of apprehended and interpreted Truth.

It is the contradiction and paradox of this day that those who seek to choke and conventionalize art, restrict and censor thought and repress imagination are demanding for their shriveled selves, freedom in precisely those lines of human activity where control and regimentation are necessary; and necessary because upon this foundation is to be built the widest conceivable freedom in a realm infinitely larger and more meaningful than the realm of economic production and distribution of wealth. The less freedom we leave for business exploitation the greater freedom we shall have for expression in art.

We have got to think of the time when poverty approaches abolition; when men no longer fear starvation and unemployment; when health is so guarded that we may normally expect to live our seventy years and more, without excess of pain and suffering. In such a world living begins; in such a world we will have freedom of thought and expression, and just as much freedom of action as maintenance of the necessary economic basis of life permits; that is, given three or six hours of work under rule and duress, we ought to be sure of at least eighteen hours of recreation, joy, and creation with a minimum of compulsion for anybody.

Freedom is the path of art, and living in the fuller and broader sense of the term is the expression of art. Yet those who speak of freedom talk usually as fools talk. So far as the laws of gravitation are concerned there can be no freedom; so far as the physical constitution of the universe is concerned, we must produce and consume goods in accordance with that which is inexorable, unmoved by sentiment or dream. But this realm of the physical need be only the smaller part of life and above it is planning, emotion and dream; in the exercising of creative power; in building, painting and literature there is a chance for the free exercise of the human spirit, broad enough and lofty enough to satisfy every ambition of the free human soul. Limited though it be by birth and death, by time and space, by health and mysterious native gift, nevertheless its realm is so magnificent that those who fear that freedom may end with the abolition of poverty or that disease is needed to insure room on the earth or that war and murder are the only handmaids of courage are all talking utter nonsense.

The freedom to create within the limits of natural law; the freedom to love without limit; the freedom to dream of the utter marriage of beauty and art; all this men may have if they are sufficiently well-bred to make human contact bearable; if they have learned to read and write and reason; if they have character enough to distinguish between right and wrong and strength enough to do right; if they can earn a decent living and know the world in which they live.

The vastest and finest truth of all, is that while wealth diminishes, by sharing and consuming and calls for control, Art, which is experience of life, increases and grows, the more widely it is shared. Here lie the rock foundations of Democracy. Selah.

So now again pass seven years. It is midnight of an autumn day; and Saint Orgne, risen beatified on the dark frustration of his soul, to the quiet peace of pain, stands in an old forest amid falling leaves, with the starry heavens above him. He knows where, months before, the heavy fragrance of purple wisteria had hallowed this air and dipped great festoons of blooms down into a scented world. But tonight these are gone. All is death. There is no sound; and yet somehow somewhere beneath lies some Tone too deep for sound—a silent chord of infinite harmony. Saint Orgne lifts his hands and waves back to the skies the seven golden candlesticks and the seven silver stars, and speaks, saying, "It is enough!" But the Voice replies:

"I see a new Heaven and a new Earth." "How can that be," wails Saint Orgne. "What is new about War and Murder? What is new in deified and organized race hate? What is new in breadlines and starvation, crime and disease? Is not our dream of Democracy done?"

The stars shine silently on, but in his own heart Saint Orgne's answer comes—Hear ye! This is the Truth of Democracy and Race.

The world compels us today as never before to examine and re-examine the problem of democracy. In theory we know it by heart: all men are equal and should have equal voice in their own government. This dictum has been vigorously attacked. All men are not equal. Ignorance cannot speak logically or clearly even when given voice. If sloth, dullness and mediocrity hold power, civilization is diluted and lowered, and government approaches anarchy. The mob cannot rule itself and will not choose the wise and able and give them the power to rule.

This attack began in 1789 during the French Revolution and it rose to crescendo some seventy years later when our fathers were enfranchised. The original dictum of human equality and the right of the governed to a voice in their government has never been universally accepted and only seldom has it been attempted. In the world today, universal suffrage is coerced by force as was true here in the South during Reconstruction; or by intimidation as was true in the South after 1876; or by economic pressure, either through threat of poverty or bribery of increased income, as has been true in the United States for years. Today finally we have entered the period of propaganda, when people to be sure may vote but cannot think freely nor clearly because of falsehood forced on their eyes and ears; or equally by the deliberate suppression of the whole truth. It is thus that there has arisen in our day, on an astonishing scale, the fascism of despair; the acquiescence of great masses of men in irresponsible tyranny, not because they want it, but because they see no other escape from greater disaster.

Let us then examine anew the basic thesis of democracy. It does not really mean to say that all men are equal; but it does assert that every individual who is a part of the state must have his experience and his necessities regarded by that state if the state survive; that the best and only ultimate authority on an individual's hurt and desire is that individual himself no matter how inarticulate his inner soul may be; that life, as any man has lived it, is part of that great national reservoir of knowledge without use of which no government can do justice.

But this is not the main end of democracy. It is not only that the complaints of all should be heard, or the hurts of the humblest healed; it is for the vastly larger object of loosing the possibilities of mankind for the development of a higher and broader and more varied human culture. Democracy then forms not merely a reservoir of complaint but of ability, hidden otherwise in poverty and ignorance. It is the astonishing result of an age of enlightenment, when the ruling classes of the world are the children of peasants, slaves and guttersnipes, that the still dominant thought is that education and ability are not today matters of chance, but mainly of individual desert and effort. As a matter of fact the chances of real ability today getting opportunity for development are not one-tenth as great as the chance of their owners dying in child-birth, being stunted by poverty or ending in prison or on the gallows. Democracy means the opening of opportunity to the disinherited to contribute to civilization and the happiness of men.

Given a chance for the majority of mankind, to be educated, healthy and free to act, it may well turn out that human equality is not so wild a dream as many seem to hope.

The intelligent democratic control of a state by its citizens does not of itself and by any mechanical formula mean good government. It must be supplemented by the thrift and unselfishness of its citizens. The citizen of a democracy who thinks of democratic government chiefly as a means of his own advancement, meets and ought to meet disappointment. Only in so far as he conceives of democracy as the only way to advance the interests of the mass of people, even when those interests conflict with his, is he playing the heroic role of a patriot. And whenever he excludes from that mass the interests of the poor and the foolish; the Jew and Negro; the Asiatic and the South Sea Islander; he kills the effort at democracy.

Democracy does not and cannot mean freedom. On the contrary it means coercion. It means submission of the individual will to the general will and it is justified in this compulsion only if the will is general and not the will of special privilege.

Far from this broad conception of democracy, we have increasingly allowed the idea to be confined to the opportunity of electing certain persons to power without regard as to whether they can or will exercise power or for what. Even this choice of the voter, in current democracies, is confined mostly to comparatively minor matters of administration; but in the great realm of making a living, the fundamental interest of all; in the matter of determining what goods shall be produced, what services shall be rendered, and how goods and services shall be shared by all, there has been deep and bitter determination, that here democracy shall never enter; that here the Tyrant or the King by the grace of God shall always and forever rule.

It is widely in vain that the basic argument for democratic control has here been brought to bear; that these goods and services are the product of the labor of the mass of men and not solely of the rich and talented; and that therefore all men must have some decisive voice in the conduct of industry and the division of wealth. To be sure this calls for more intelligence, technical knowledge of intricate facts and forces, and greater will to work and sacrifice than most men today have; which is only saying that the mass of men must more and more largely acquire this knowledge, skill and character; and that meantime its wide absence is no valid excuse of surrendering the control of industry to the anarchy of greed and the tyranny of chance.

This faces us directly with our problem in America. Our best brains are taught and want to be taught in large northern universities where dominant economic patterns and European culture, not only prevail, but prevail almost to the exclusion of anything else.

Naturally these men are then grabbed up with rolling eyes and eager mien by the best Southern Negro schools. Now if these Negro universities have any real meaning it is that in them other points of view should be evolved. They may or may not be radically different. They may bring something entirely new or be an adaptation of surrounding civilization; but certainly they should logically bring a newness of view and a re-examination of the old, of the European, and of the white, which would be stimulating and which would be real education.

But right here we have not simply little or no advance, but we have attitudes which make advance impossible. On the matter of race, for instance, we are ultra-modern. There are certainly no biological races in the sense of people with large groups of unvarying inherited gifts and instincts thus set apart by nature as eternally separate. We have seen the whole world reluctantly but surely approaching this truth. We have therefore hastened to conclude there is no sense in studying racial subjects or inculcating racial ideals or writing racial textbooks or projecting vocational guidance from the point of view of race. And yet standing in stark contradiction of all this are the surrounding facts of race: the Jim Crow seats on the street cars every day, the Jim Crow coaches on the railroads, the separate sections of the city where the races dwell; the discrimination in occupations and opportunities and in law; and beyond that the widespread division of the world by custom into white, yellow, and black, ruler and eternally ruled.

We American Negroes form and long will form a perfectly definite group, not entirely segregated and isolated from our surroundings, but differentiated to such a degree that we have very largely a life and thought of our own. And it is this fact that we as scientists, and teachers and persons engaged in living, earning a living, have got to take into account and make our major problem. In the face of that, we have these young intellectual exquisites who smile if they do not laugh outright at our writhings. Their practical program is so far as our race or group is concerned: Do nothing, think nothing, become absorbed in the nation.

To which the flat answer is: this is impossible. We have got to do something about race. We have got to think and think clearly about our present situation. Absorption into the nation, save as a long, slow intellectual process, is unthinkable and while it may eventually come, its trend and result depends very largely upon what kind of a group is being absorbed; whether such racial integration has to do with poverty-stricken and half-starved criminals; or whether with intelligent self-guided, independently acting men, who know what they want and propose at any civilized cost to get it. No, separated and isolated as we are so largely, we form in America an integral group, call it by any name you will, and this fact in itself has its meaning, its worth and its values.

In no line is this clearer than in the democratization of industry. We are still a poor people, a mass of laborers, with few rich folk and little exploitation of labor. We can be among the first to help restore the idea of high culture and limited income and dispel the fable that riotous wealth alone is civilization. Acting together, voluntarily or by outer compulsion, we can be the units through which universal democracy may be accomplished.

We black folk have striven to be Americans. And like all other Americans, we have longed to become rich Americans. Wealth comes easiest today through the exploitation of labor by paying low wages; and if we have not widely exploited our own and other labor the praise belongs not to us, but to those whites whose monopoly of wealth and ruthless methods have out-run our tardy and feeble efforts. This is the place to pause and look about, as well, backward as forward. The leaders of the labor movement in America as in Europe, deceived us just as they deceived themselves. They left us out. They paid no attention to us, whether we were drudging in colonies or slaving in cotton fields or pleading in vain at the door of union labor factories. The object of white labor was not the uplift of all labor; it was to join capital in sharing the loot from exploited colored labor. So we too, only half emancipated, hurled ourselves forward, too willing if it had but been possible, to climb up to a bourgeois heaven on the prone bodies of our fellows. But white folk occupied and crowded these stairs. And white labor loved the white exploiter of black folk far more than it loved its fellow black proletarian.

Such is the plight of democracy today. Where in this picture does the American Negro come? With few exceptions, we are all today "white folks' niggers." No, do not wince. I mean nothing insulting or derogatory, but this is a concrete designation which indicates that very very many colored folk: Japanese, Chinese, Indians, Negroes; and, of course, the vast majority of white folk; have been so enthused, oppressed, and suppressed by current white civilization that they think and judge everything by its terms. They have no norms that are not set in the nineteenth and twentieth centuries. They can conceive of no future world which is not dominated by present white nations and thoroughly shot through with their ideals, their method of government, their economic organization, their literature and their art; or in other words their throttling of democracy, their exploitation of labor, their industrial imperialism and their color hate. To broach before such persons any suggestion of radical change; any idea of intrusion, physical or spiritual, on the part of alien races is to bring down upon one's devoted head the most tremendous astonishment and contempt.

What to do? We went to school. But our industrial schools taught no industrial history, no labor movement, no social reform,—only technique just when the technique of skilled trades was changing to mass industry. Our colleges taught the reactionary economics of Northern schools. We landed in bitter and justifiable complaint and sought a way out by complaining. Our mistake lay not in the injustice of our cause, but in our naive assumption that a system of industrial monopoly that was making money out of our exploitation, was going voluntarily to help us escape its talons.

On the other hand when we turn to join the forces of progress and reform we find again no easy or obvious path. As the disinherited both of labor and capital; as those discriminated against by employer and employee, we are forced to a most careful and thorough-going program of minority planning. We may call this self-segregation if we will but the compulsion is from without and inevitable. We may call it racial chauvinism but we may make it the path to democracy through group culture. This path includes sympathy and cooperation with the labor movement; with the efforts of those who produce wealth, to assert their right to control it. It has been no easy path. What with organized, intelligent and powerful opposition and ignorant and venal and dogmatic leadership, the white labor movement has staggered drunkenly for two hundred years or more and yet it has given the world a vision of real democracy, of universal education and of a living wage. It is the most promising movement of modern days and we who are primarily laborers must eventually join it.

In addition to this, no matter how great our political disfranchisement and social exclusion, we have in our hands a voting power which is enormous, and that is the control we can exercise over the production and distribution of goods through our expenditure as consumers. The might and efficiency of this method of economic reform is continually minimized by the obvious fact that it does not involve radical change and that without other and more thorough-going changes it can bring no immediate millenium. But notwithstanding for a minority group it is the most powerful weapon at hand and to refuse to use an instrument of power because it is not all powerful is silly.

A people who buy each year at least a half billion dollars worth of goods and services are not helpless. If they starve it is their own fault. If they do not achieve a respected place in the surrounding industrial organization, it is because they are stupid.

Here then is the plight and the steps toward remedy. Yet we are not awake. We have let obvious opportunities slip by during these awful days of depression when we have lost much of the land we used to own; when our savings have been dissipated; when our business enterprises have failed and when if not a majority a strikingly large minority of us are existing on public charity. We have not asked for the advantage of public housing as we should. We have not taken advantage of the possibilities of the TVA. We have not pushed energetically into plans of re-settlement and the establishment of model villages. We have almost refused the subsistence homestead. We have not begun to think of socialized medicine and consumers cooperation. We have no comprehensive plans concerning our unemployment, our economic dependence, the profit economy and the changing technique of industry. The day of our reckoning is at hand. Awake, awake, put on thy strength oh Zion.

The martyrdom of man may be increased and prolonged through primitive, biological racial propaganda, but on the other hand through cooperation, education and understanding the cultural race unit may be the pipe line through which human civilization may extend to wider and wider areas to the fertilization of mankind.

It is to this use of our racial unity and loyalty that the United States impels us. We cannot escape it. Only through racial effort today can we achieve economic stability, cultural growth and human understanding. The way to democracy lies through race loyalty if only that is its real and consciously comprehended end. Selah and Amen.

This then is the revelation of Saint Orgne the Damned, as given me by his hand; and the philosophy of life out of which he strove to climb, despite the curse, to broader and more abundant life. Bearing this revelation, men and women of the Class of 1938, there return to you today, three pilgrims, and the ghosts of three others, whose memories await us. Fifty years ago we stood where you stand and received the Light of the Seven Stars. We return, not all-wise, but wise; for we have seen ten presidents rule in America and five kings reign in England; we have seen the fall of three great empires; a whole world at war to commit twenty-six million murders; the rise of dark Japan and fall of darker Ethiopia. We have seen our own race in America nearly double in number from less than seven to more than twelve million souls.

We return home today worn and travel stained, yet with the Light which Alma Mater laid upon our hands; it does not burn so high nor flash so fiercely—yet it has lighted thousands of other candles, and it is still aflame. We hand it on to you, that fifty years hence you give it again to others—and so on forever.

ENVOY

No final word is really necessary. These speeches are snap-shots of my mental states over a period of thirty-two years, a generation of man. They vary from the narrowness of intense conviction to the vagueness of doctrines that attempt universality. They have, however, as I have said before, a certain historic significance. They tell from one point of view, what the American Negro has thought of that education which was designed to fit him as a citizen of modern democracy.

[The text as originally structured by Du Bois in 1940 ends here.—HA]

Editor's Note

In correspondence with the Director of the University of North Carolina Press, while consideration was still being given to the publishing of the manuscript of "Seven Critiques," Du Bois suggested the possibility of including the 1941 essay that follows. Again, in 1943, he inquired of publishers Reynal and Hitchcock if there would be an interest in a volume of his writings on education, but the response was negative.

Included here with this 1941 essay are an address delivered in 1946, as the postwar world was commencing, and another delivered in 1960 when Du Bois was in his tenth decade and when his astonishing life was clearly nearing its end.

The 1941 address, "The Future of the Negro State University," was delivered as the Founders' Day Address at Lincoln University in Jefferson City, Missouri on January 12, 1941. Governor L. C. Stark of Missouri spoke briefly prior to Du Bois. The latter's remarks were extensively reported in the Black press—such as the *Philadelphia Tribune*, January 23, 1941. The complete address, with corrections made by Du Bois, appeared soon after (in the *Wilberforce University Quarterly*, April 1941; 2:53–60).

"The Future and Function of the Private Negro College" was delivered at the seventy-first anniversary Commencement exercises of Knoxville College in Tennessee on June 10, 1946. The corrected manuscript was published in the *Crisis* (August 1946; 53:234–36, 253–54). Du Bois had returned in 1944 to work with the NAACP, as Director of Special Research, and so the appearance of his remarks in the association's organ was in no way unusual.

By the end of 1947, however, Du Bois and the NAACP again parted company, largely because of Du Bois's intense anti-colonialism and his growing opposition to dominant tendencies manifested by the Truman Administration, especially in foreign affairs. In 1948 began his association with the Council on African Affairs—and with Paul Robeson and W. Alphaeus Hunton, in particular—and somewhat later with the world-wide peace movement, which culminated in Du Bois's leadership of the Peace Information Center.

With the end of the 1940s and the decade of the 1950s, Du Bois was a central opponent of the growing drift towards the Right in the United States which eventuated in McCarthyism. In 1950 he ran in New York for the United States Senate, on the ticket of the American Labor Party (and received about 200,000 votes); the next year he was tried, under the McCormick Act, as an "unregistered foreign agent" and was acquitted. Thereafter his identification with the Left was complete and he became, along with Paul Robeson, an unmentionable name in the dominant media.

While the boycott extended to sections of the Black population and institutions, it was nowhere as complete there. Reflecting this fact was the invitation extended to Du Bois early in 1960 to address the twenty-fifth Conference of the Association of [Black] Social Science Teachers. For the occasion he prepared the paper "Whither Now and Why," and it was delivered at the conference, held at Johnson C. Smith University in Charlotte, North Carolina, on April 2, 1960. At this time, Du Bois was in his ninety-second year. His paper was published in the *Quarterly Review of Higher Education among Negroes* (July 1960; 28:135–41).

The Future of the Negro State University

It is significant that the institution whose seventy-fifth anniversary we are celebrating today arose out of this chain of circumstances. It was among the black soldiers of Missouri fighting the last battle of the West which spelled the final crippling of the Confederacy that the idea arose of systematic education of their fellows in their home state. Nor was there anything unusual or merely local in this thought and movement. The public school system of the whole South is the gift of black folk. An element in the white South had struggled for a public school system and had sought to follow New England and the West in this direction long before the Civil War, but it is a needless exaggeration to say that there was in the confines of the former slave states, south of Mason and Dixon's line, any real state public school system until the black votes of Reconstruction furnished one. Even in the Middlewest, Ohio, Illinois, Indiana, and Missouri, the public school system did not usually include or envisage Negroes, and it was only when Missouri colored troops saw with their own eyes what Negroes were doing for public education in Louisiana and Texas that they sent back the idea to their own state.

The new democratic state which thus arose north and south after the Civil War was hampered and curtailed in its power. Especially its effort to regulate industry and control wages failed ignominiously; but the consequent demand for *light and more light,* for wider and deeper understanding of human processes showed itself in a new attitude toward popular education and consequently toward Negro education.

I was brought up in a day and state where education beyond the grammar school, beyond elementary reading, writing, and arithmetic, was considered to be a private matter. If a child was to be educated in the high school and college and for the professions, this was a matter to which the private individual and private fortunes should attend. This was the New England

129

counterpart of the English idea of education which lasted there down almost to our day.

There grew up consequently in New England endowed high schools and private colleges which have become the best known in the nation and which long prided themselves on giving training not simply to the rich and well-to-do but even to talented children of all classes and races. I can remember that the first catalogue of Harvard University which I ever saw had in it a statement that the "experience of the university warrants the sentence that no student of ability need leave the institution because of lack of funds." [1] This situation gradually changed. The demand for high school and college training on the part of the mass of youth in the United States rapidly outran the facilities which private institutions supported by private endowments could furnish, and there arose the public town and city high school and the state university. The voting masses of Americans demanded vastly expanded opportunities for learning. These facilities have grown so rapidly and expanded so enormously in work and attendance that it is manifest that by the twenty-first century the problem of higher education is going to be primarily a problem of the state.

This fills some folks with satisfaction and others with dismay, because it puts into the hands of the state the necessity of facing and facing squarely certain social situations and problems which the state as it is now constituted has not shown itself capable of handling. Not only is there the older problems of religion and social status but what are today the much more pressing problems of class distinction based on income and of racial distinctions based on physical differences and appearances and on historical associations supported by prejudice and folklore.

1. The *Harvard University Catalogue,* 1888–89 (published by the University, Cambridge, 1888), p. 142, states: "The experience of the past warrants the statement that good scholars of high character but slender means are very rarely obliged to leave the College for want of money." For several years thereafter an identical or substantially similar statement appeared in the catalogue.

The new state system of education, therefore, is faced first of all with this question of income, this question which the democratic experiments following the Civil War attempted to meet and failed. It is all well enough to talk about equality of human beings and their liberty to act; the real fact of the matter, as we have known for generations and as we are beginning to admit today, is that a man who does not have enough to eat or the clothing and shelter necessary for health, and who is uncertain as to how long his present meagre income is going to last, is not free, and cannot be called the equal of the man with sufficient and assured income and security of status. The comfortable solution of this economic problem which regards this situation as largely inevitable and which looks upon poverty as the permanent accompaniment of civilization is not only being questioned today, but is the real burning problem which lay at the basis of the last World War and is the cause of this present World War and of other revolutions to come. The solution of attitudes toward this economic problem is in the long run in the hands of our educational system, and it goes without saying that the present educational system is not designed to meet it. It is a system largely determined by that very economic inequality which it seeks to solve; and the power to administer the system lies all too largely in hands interested in privilege rather than in justice and in class advantage rather than in democratic control.

If this were all, the problem of state education would be a most difficult one. But, in addition to this, we have here in the United States problems of race and culture concentrated in our vast cities, concentrated in the rural districts of the Southern South and forming a considerable and difficult problem in border regions like this. This set of problems includes minorities of various types, vestiges of religious controversies stemming from other days, remainders of extreme economic inequalities as represented by various migratory groups, differences due to physique and appearance and, above all, differences due to cultural history. Indeed, the whole civilized world today is a mass of race controversies and contacts bound up with all mankind.

Among these you and I especially are victims of those so-called racial problems which range themselves about the history of slavery in this country, and which have left us, some twelve or more millions of people more or less of African descent, of varying cultures and different degrees of education, who stand out, not simply because of visible differences in appearance, but because of historical differences due to their cultural and economic inheritance. They are, for instance, in large majority, poor people with small income. They are ignorant people having been until quite recently deprived of education; and they are associated in the public mind, through the reiteration of the printed word and the pictured fact, with inferiority and lack of ability. The problem of the education of these persons must be faced by state systems of training, and this problem is being faced with every conceivable difference of attitude varying from open and careless neglect to desperate and often misguided efforts at solution.

In a state like this the usual attitude long has been to resent the fact that such a problem must complicate the policies of the state system of education. It could of course easily be argued that the simpler the problems of education are, the easier it would be to solve them; that if a state school system had to deal with persons of about the same income status, the same cultural background and comparatively few physical differences, the resultant problem of education would be easy. Perhaps so, but certainly it would not be a problem of education suited to this nation or this world. This is a world where the physical, mental, and cultural differences between human beings are vast; where the absolute segregation of human beings is increasingly impossible and undesirable; where the annihilation of space, the economic interdependence of peoples, and the necessary political cooperation are such that no problem of education in any country can long hope to escape the resultant questions of facts of human contact. It has indeed been thought in theory at least that one of the great advantages of the United States lay in the very combination and contacts of people which our polyglot citizenship and political organization involved. But even those who advocated this theory were apt to shy a bit here and there at the Irish and the Germans, at Italians and Mexicans, at the Jews and the Slovaks, at Asiatics of all sorts, and, of course, at Negroes.

So admitting today that the state system of education has got to regard the different elements in the state as an inescapable part of its problem, we come to the second situation: namely, that as an heritage from slavery and the Civil War we are required by state law to carry on separate institutions for persons of Negro descent. There is no doubt that this is unfortunate and even idiotic. It is needlessly costly and it is a direct contravention to that democratic equality toward which all education in the end must strive. And yet so far as these laws reflect a real state of mind; so far as they simply put into words deeper than feelings, will, and determination on the part of the dominant group that co-education of the races is a thing more to be feared than the failure of democracy or even of life itself; so far as this remains true or even seems true such a situation has got to be faced.

There is, of course, in everyone's mind the conviction that such inherited prejudice, largely the result of unconscious and subconscious psychological reactions, is not and cannot be permanent. But it is a difficult matter to say just when and where the end of such prejudice can be looked for or assumed. One would think that, in a state like Missouri where Negroes form but one-sixth of the population and where the actual illiteracy of whites and blacks is not great, time and a reasonable amount of tolerance would make the waste and duplication of work necessary in two state universities uncalled for; and that a little patient waiting and thoughtful pressure might even in our day have opened the doors of the University of Missouri to colored students.

In the meantime, however, there were certain losses which could hardly be faced. The admission of a few colored students to the University of Missouri would not alter the mental complexion of the teachers and professors in that institution. They would know as little about the cultural history and group difficulties of Negro students after as before. Even in large national institutions like the University of Chicago, the University of Illinois, the University of Indiana, Yale, Harvard, and Columbia, colored students have undergone enormous disadvantages and unconscious as well as deliberate discrimination because their white teachers were systematically ignorant of the place of the Negro in human culture. Whole sections of human history have been slurred over or misinterpreted; science has been systematically distorted to prove a prejudice; and above all most of these teachers have refused to visualize the possibility of a Negro becoming a full self-respecting American citizen.

Last year, in the University of Pennsylvania, a Negro student of fine physique, excellent family, and unusual ability elected a course under a well-known professor in the social sciences. The professor called him in and said to him, "Blank, I have heard of your work and I know that you are a good student but I want to tell you frankly and openly that I have such prejudice against Negroes that I could not treat you fairly in my classes. If under those circumstances you want to take this course, all right." The student quietly withdrew. This man and this case were exceptional, but there are dozens of white teachers in white universities who only differ from this one in being less frank.

Whether then it was inevitable or not, Missouri has embarked upon the road of establishing a Negro university and of making that institution a center of learning and scientific advance deserving to be classed as the equal of other universities in this land. That, of course, is a difficult job. First of all, any time that a state is compelled by higher law or by lower prejudice to embark upon a program for which it has no real liking, the work will be done, at first certainly, in a cheap and slipshod way. The separate institution will be by all standards a poor institution: poor in physical equipment, poor in cultural advantages, tempted to imitate where it cannot be real, and to boast of what it has not.

Any Negro institution will have natural difficulty in calling to its service persons thoroughly trained for the kind of work which they will have to do. Just because a man is black does not make him a scholar nor a teacher. Having been called to teach, such persons will usually be paid at a rate with which no white man would or ought to be satisfied. They will be given less security of tenure, fewer surroundings of the larger life, and less of honor and spiritual satisfaction. Such a situation will call for unusual sacrifice and devotion on the part of teachers and rare loyalty on the part of students; no one of these things necessarily comes for the asking or the need. They must be built up by unusual strains and stresses and by loyalties which may in themselves become dangerous.

Inevitably among a poor and inexperienced people, the temptation will come and recur to make an institution like this, a means of earning a living or of adding to income rather than an institution of learning. The Negroes of Missouri will be tempted in the future, as in the past, to sell their votes not for the establishment of a state university but for small offices and temporary preferment, for the paying of personal debts and squaring of personal dislikes and enmities, rather than for the larger and more intangible object of building here a center of thought and speculation, of scientific research, and of literature and art. Every state university in this nation has gone through this period of petty politics and some are still passing through it. It is only by the hardest effort and the deepest sacrifice and devotion to the greater life that a group and a state can rise to the high conception of what a university can do and what it may be, and what place it should occupy in a democracy.

There is always the problem of what an institution like this should aim at. Should Lincoln University try to become another University of Missouri? After all, among the great universities of America, the University of Missouri would hardly be placed among the first. It can be considered a sort of average of those plodding miscellaneous centers of crowds, dispensing an education with varying degrees of efficiency. Lincoln University has before it certain obvious differences of method and aim: it can and should be smaller and more compact; it can be more certain of its object and more definite and thorough in its methods. There are certain lines of work in which it can stand out, not simply in Missouri, but in the United States as a focus of research and as a place of culture and civilization for a new and evolving world. You have an extraordinary opportunity, not so much for social imitation and social conflict, but rather for social invention, for planning and carrying through methods by which, without hatred, agitation, or upheaval, you can show how a minority can not simply repeat the accomplishments of a majority, but can show the majority the way of life. In doing this, you but reiterate an age-old custom that not from the overwhelming, rich, and powerful groups which from time to time rule the world have come salvation and culture, but from the still small voice of the oppressed and the determined who knew more than to die and plan more than mere survival.

But for this, Lincoln will need freedom and funds. It will need to be administered by men of large vision who think of this school not as a temporary make-shift or as a place where their relatives get positions or their firms sell goods, but rather as a center where the cultural outlook of this country is to be changed and uplifted and helped in the reconstruction of the world.

Lincoln University has already come a long road in this direction. I can remember that forty-seven years ago I received a letter from what was then Lincoln Institute, asking me to be a member of its faculty and promising me a salary considerably larger than that for which I had promised to work at Wilberforce. I refused the invitation almost without second thought, because the Lincoln Institute of that day had an unsavory reputation. It was a center of graft, of low ideals, of inefficient work. It was well-known that no president could stay here who was not a politician of resource, and teachers held their positions only by careful negotiation with the trustees and the political bosses of the state. From that time, Lincoln Institute, now Lincoln University, has come a long way, but it has a long way still to go. It has not altogether been freed of its purely political relations, but that is true of many other state institutions of higher learning throughout the United States, white and black. But there has been a change, and after seventy-five years of most difficult effort and self-sacrificing strife one begins to see the chance of establishing a real university here; a Negro university not in the sense that it is teaching Negro science or merely Negro history or Negro mathematics, but in the larger and broader sense that here science and education are being so followed that the place of the Negro in the world and his relation to the body of his fellow human beings is being made clear; and a fertile starting point prepared for a democracy of human culture which will make peace in the world not only possible but profitable for all men.

This university and its dark fellows in the land are not simply American; they are inter-national and part of a new world pattern of which Negroes are thinking. For, "What do Negroes themselves think of these their problems and the attitude of the world toward them?" First and most significant: They are thinking. There is as yet no great single centralizing of thought or unification of opinion, but there are centers which are growing larger and touching edges. The most significant centers of this new thinking are, perhaps naturally, outside Africa and in America: in the United States and in the West Indies; this is followed by South Africa and West Africa and then, more vaguely, by South America, with faint beginnings in East Central Africa, Nigeria, and the Sudan.

The Pan-African movement when it comes will not, however, be merely a narrow racial propaganda. Already the more far-seeing Negroes sense the coming unities: a unity of the working classes everywhere, a unity of the colored races, a new unity of thinking men. The economic solution of the Negro problem in Africa and America has turned the thoughts of Negroes toward a realization of the fact that the modern white laborer of Europe and America has the key to serfdom of black folk in his support of militarism and colonial expansion. He is beginning to say to these workingmen that so long as black laborers are slaves white laborers cannot be free. Already there are signs in South Africa and the United States of the beginning of understanding between the two classes.

In a conscious sense of unity among colored races there is

today only a growing interest. There is slowly arising not only a curiously strong brotherhood of Negro blood throughout the world, but the common cause of the darker races against the intolerable assumptions and insults of Europeans has already found expression. Most men in this world are colored. A belief in humanity means a belief in colored men. The future world will, in all reasonable probability, be what colored men make it. In order for this colored world to come into its heritage, must the earth be continuously drenched in the blood of fighting, snarling human beasts? Or will reason and good-will prevail? That the latter may be true, the character of the Negro race is the best and greatest hope; for in its normal condition it is at once the strongest and gentlest of the races of men, but that character can only be raised, above emotion to planned reason by institutions such as this may become.

The Future and Function of
the Private Negro College

We all know the main lines of the rise of Negro education in the United States: after a desperate and sporadic struggle to finance and maintain Negro schools, resulting in several
schools among free Negroes north and south and in two schools
of higher training before the Civil War, there came after emancipation, a mass demand for popular education unequalled by
any other group in world history. Of how that demand was met
I wrote forty years ago in *The Souls of Black Folk:*

> Through the shining trees that whisper before me as I
> write, I catch glimpses of a boulder of New England
> granite, covering a grave, which graduates of Atlanta
> University have placed there, with this inscription: "In
> grateful memory of this former teacher and friend and
> of the unselfish life he lived, and the noble work he
> wrought; that they, their children, and their children's
> children might be blessed."
>
> This was the gift of New England to the freed Negro;
> not alms, but a friend; not cash, but character. It was
> not and is not money these seething millions want, but
> love and sympathy, the pulse of hearts beating with red
> blood—a gift which today only their own kindred and
> race can bring to the masses, but which once saintly
> souls brought to their favored children in the crusade of
> the sixties, that finest thing in American history, and
> one of the few things untainted by sordid greed and
> cheap vainglory. The teachers in these institutions came
> not to keep the Negroes in their place, but to raise them
> out of the defilement of the places where slavery had
> wallowed them. The colleges they founded were social
> settlements; homes where the best of the sons of the
> freedom came in close and sympathetic touch with the
> best traditions of New England. They lived and ate
> together, studied and worked, hoped and harkened in
> the dawning light. In actual formal content their

curriculum was doubtless old-fashioned, but in educational power it was supreme, for it was the contact of living souls.

Since those days these colleges have gone through various transitions. For a while they had to support themselves by contributions chiefly from the missionary funds of Northern churches and from federal funds which Negroes provided. Then for twenty-five years they tried to raise larger sums from philanthropists, often from prosperous sons of the original teachers and founders. Later the colored colleges turned toward the state for aid. Today the private institutions are facing the fact that unless they receive increased contributions, not now in sight, and these funds reach large figures, they must either close or become fully state schools.

I have in many cases urged that the state must in the future support and control higher education because of its large and increasing cost. The church today carries, or should carry, too heavy a burden of social duties to permit it to continue to support large and increasingly expensive colleges. With almost unanimous action, they are shifting this burden to public appropriation or private philanthropy. This means of course less religious influence in colleges, which has both its good and bad side. I said at Wilberforce only a few years ago that the only visible future for that first of Negro colleges was to become a state school. Private philanthropy as a support of higher education is undesirable, as I shall point out later.

There are in the United States today one hundred and eighteen Negro colleges giving from one to four years of college work. Thirty-six of these are supported by government funds, chiefly from the United States and the states. Eighty-two are supported by private organizations. In 1940 these colleges were attended by about 45,000 students and 28,000 of these were in schools of A or B grading, meaning that they were doing fairly efficient college work.

These colleges receive considerably more than $15 million a year in income of which $9 million at least goes to the private colleges. But the source of this income has been varying in instructive ways during the generation from 1910 to 1940. In 1910, for instance, private institutions received less than a fifth of their income from student fees while today they receive nearly a third from fees; indicating the marked economic progress of Negroes which enables them today to pay a considerable share of the expense of educating their children. When I was at Fisk in the years from 1884 to 1888, there was not a single college student who was able to pay ten per cent of the fees.

The contribution from endowment funds, furnished chiefly by philanthropists has not varied much, ranging from 38 to 46 per cent. There are indications that this source may dwindle in the near future because endowments are not eternal and can only be depended upon for relatively short priods. This is a reversal of our economic beliefs in the nineteenth century. Led on by British capitalism, founded on Negro slavery, we assumed that income from a given batch of invested capital would if rightly administered continue forever. This we now realize is false and evil. Wealth for consumption or future use is no more eternal than the muscle or brain which created it and can only last forever by continuing to take from wages and giving to profit an absolutely unjustifiable share. It is on this fact that the whole argument for more equitable distribution of production rests. Consequently we see endowments of all sorts dwindling, and richly endowed institutions continually appealing for more funds. Three-fourths of my communications from Harvard since my graduation in 1890, have been appeals for contributions.

But the most serious fact is that while the private institutions got nearly one-half their support from gifts in 1910, they got only a fifth of that support from gifts in 1940. What now are these institutions going to do? Some of them have begun to turn and are turning increasingly to state aid. Of the sixteen leading private Negro colleges Tuskegee, Wilberforce, and probably Lincoln (Pennsylvania) are doubtless going to get their income increasingly from the state. Certain of the smaller church schools such as Clark, Paine, Morris Brown and Shaw, cannot hope for larger contributions from the church and must, therefore, explore other methods of support.

Atlanta University, as a graduate school, has adequate funds from endowment just now to meet its present needs but it will not have twenty years from now for an expanding future. There are certain other schools such as Talladega, Morehouse, Dillard, Fisk, Knoxville and Virginia Union which were formerly church schools, but have already outgrown that support and the problem of their future is serious. Xavier will, of course, continue to be supported by the Catholic Church for reasons not entirely educational.

Two questions, therefore, present themselves: are these institutions worth saving? Especially, is this last group of six private institutions without adequate or any church support worth saving or is their fate either to become state schools or disappear?

First it is clear that they cannot hope for support from miscellaneous and philanthropic gifts and this would be undesirable even if it were possible. Education is not and should not be a private philanthropy: it is a public service and whenever it becomes merely a gift of the rich it is in danger. Probably the greatest threat to American education today is the fact that its great and justly celebrated private institutions are supported mainly by their rich graduates: Harvard, Yale, Columbia, Princeton together with smaller institutions like Amherst and Williams are increasingly looked upon as belonging to a certain class in American society: the 'class of the rich, well-to-do employers, whose interests are more or less openly opposed to those of the laboring millions. It is because of this unfortunate situation that the clear unhampered study of the industrial process and of economic science has made so little progress in the United States at a time when the critical situation of the modern world calls desperately for such knowledge and teaching.

In the same way and for something of the same reasons the state institutions are often inhibited from development of the economic and social sciences because of political influence and because of wealth and class working through politics. But here is the hope of the democratic process; as democracy replaces oligarchy in industry, concurrently, the social and educational work of the state will improve in object and method. We can see evidence of this in state universities like Wisconsin and Michigan. On the other hand in southern states like Texas, the state university has been the football of the oil interests. Negro state colleges were a generation ago hot-beds of graft for white politicians; only in the last ten years have they been able to begin to develop a decent educational program.

In the long interim, while the state is gathering strength and democratic authority for its educational duties, and perhaps long after that, may not there be a field in the private college for a certain educational leadership and individuality? And particularly in a distinct social group, like that of the American Negro, may there not be a peculiar function for the Negro private colleges which no other social organ could fill? There would certainly seem to be a distinct place in the educational world for some private institutions whose support is such that they would be free to teach what they thought ought to be taught, particularly in the critical and developing field of social investigation.

If this is true of colleges in general, it is equally true for the same and additional reasons in the Negro college. We American Negroes are not simply Americans, or simply Negroes. We form a minority group in a great vast conglomerated land and a minority group which by reason of its efforts during the last two generations has made extraordinary and gratifying progress. But in the making of this progress, in the working together of peoples belonging to this group, in the patterns of thinking which they have had to follow and the memories which they shared, they have built-up a distinct and unique culture, a body of habit, thought and adjustment which they cannot escape because it is in the marrow of their bones and which they ought not to ignore because it is the only path to a successful future.

What is a culture? It is a careful Knowledge of the Past out of which the group as such has emerged: in our case a knowledge of African history and social development—one of the richest and most intriguing which the world has known. Our history in America, north, south and Caribbean, has been an extraordinary one which we must know to understand ourselves and our world. The experience through which our ancestors have gone for four hundred years is part of our bone and sinew whether we know it or not. The methods which we evolved for opposing slavery and fighting prejudice are not to be forgotten, but learned for our own and others' instruction. We must understand the differences in social problems between Africa, the West Indies, South and Central America, not only among the Negroes but those affecting Indians and other minority groups. Plans for the future of our group must be built on a base of our problems, our dreams and frustrations; they cannot stem from empty air or successfully be based on the experiences of others alone. The problem of our children is distinctive: when shall a colored child learn of the color line? At home, at school or suddenly on the street? What shall we do in art and literature? Shall we seek to ignore our background and graft ourselves on a culture which does not wholly admit us, or build anew on that marvellous African art heritage, one of the world's greatest as all critics now admit? Whence shall our drama come, from ourselves today or from Shakespeare in the English seventeenth century?

Many Negroes do not realize this. In their haste to become Americans, their desire not to be peculiar or segregated in mind or body, they try to escape their cultural heritage and the body of experience which they themselves have built-up. This is the reason that there is always a certain risk in taking a colored student from his native environment and transplanting him suddenly to a northern school. He may adjust himself, he may through the help of his own social group in the neighborhood of this school successfully achieve an education through the facilities offered. On the other hand he may meet peculiar frustration and in the end be unable to achieve success in the new environment or fit into the old.

For these and analogous reasons I am convinced that there is a place and a continuing function for the small Negro college. This is additional reason that this college should have a certain kind of independent support. If a number of small colleges with one or less than two hundred students, with a carefully selected faculty and clearly conceived methods and ideals could survive in America, they might have unusual opportunity to fill a great need and to do a work which no other agency could do so well. They would not be subservient to the dominant wealth of the country; they would not be under the control of politics in a state now directed for the most part by prejudiced persons guided by a definite ideal of racial discrimination.

The question then comes: how can such schools be supported and what would their program be? It was estimated in that very excellent *National Survey of Higher Education of Negroes* made by the United States Office of Education in 1940 that the cost of educating a student in a small private college was about $452 a year in addition to housing and board. If we put this total cost at $900, it would probably be true that Negro students could pay from one-fourth to a third of this cost. At $600 a student a small college then would cost $120,000 a year to which must be added something for buildings, grounds, a broad program of free scholarships and other items of administration which might bring the total cost to $150,000. Extra gifts for buildings, emergencies, and scholarships might still come from church, liberal donors or even the state; the main source of current maintenance must be the organized alumni.

How now could a small college raise $150,000 outside of what the students pay? There is, of course, but one method and that is for the alumni and the local constituency of the college to tax themselves for this amount. A college with two thousand graduates could raise this sum rather easily if each graduate gave $100 a year not as a pledge but as an actual payment. This amounts to two dollars a week. If the college had only one thousand graduates it would amount to four dollars a week, I say "tax" and I mean tax: a payment as regular and recognized as just as compulsory as any tax.

The question comes, therefore, could the graduates of such colleges be made to see vividly enough the necessity of their continued existence so that they would be willing to tax themselves to this considerable amount. I believe it would be possible but only possible if this kind of contribution was lifted out of the class of ordinary miscellaneous giving to which we are so used and stressed throughout the college course as an absolute necessity for the maintenance of independent methods of education. This would be an innovation. I am not sure that we have in our student body today and our body of graduates the guts for any such real sacrifice. We are used to being educated for nothing and expecting praise for giving our valuable time. We pay on the nail for spring clothes, automobiles, and golf clubs, but for a college training? I do not know.

What now should such a college be and what should it do? It should in the first place be small. We should get rid of the idea of bigness which permeates American ideals. A college of two thousand students is an entirely different kind of institution from a college of one hundred students. The success and marked success of Fisk and Talladega and Atlanta and similar institutions in earlier years was the fact that their college department consisted of a small number of students brought into direct contact for long periods with able teachers. When I first went to Atlanta University to teach there were only twenty-five students in college and the whole college department at Fisk during my undergraduate days consisted of less than twenty persons. What is needed for efficient education of youth is individual attention, close acquaintanceship with their fellows and that skilled guidance that only can be gotten in the small college.

Secondly, this college must have a carefully selected faculty; its president must be not a financier and collector of funds but an educational administrator capable of laying down an educational program and selecting the people who can carry it out. The teachers in such a college must be scholars and gentlemen: scholars in the sense of having direct and careful acquaintanceship with modern science and gentlemen in the sense of knowing and practicing the highest canons of good taste and conduct. The curriculum of a college of this sort would be comparatively simple: the idea of acquainting growing youth with what the world has known in science and art and what it is doing today; and in making that acquaintanceship as complete and thorough as time allows; the idea of knowing thoroughly the lives of people today, comparing them with the people of the past and evolving through science a guide and prophet for the future.

For this reason the college should be equipped with library, laboratories, a museum and an art gallery. The library should contain the body of human life and experience in such quantity and number as to be easily and quickly accessible to all; it should be conducted by persons who know the inside of books better than their backs and catalogue numbers. The college should have a theatre for the drama and facilities for hearing and studying music. But above and beyond this it should have a distinct department of adult education calculated to teach its students from the first the art of reading and writing. Most of the students who come to college, white and black all over the United States, do not read and write well. And many who come to our colleges cannot read and write at all. The reason for this does not necessarily involve any individual blame. It is because of the wretched system of public schools where these students have been trained. The system of elementary education in the United States has got to be improved and in the end will be; but in the meantime one or two generations of students will grow-up and will have to know how to read and write and cipher in order to pursue a college course. Each college, therefore, should have provision for the scientific teaching of reading, writing and arithmetic to adult persons. The experience of the army in this war has shown that this is a perfectly feasible program.

Finally a main object of such a college should be vocational guidance. So much nonsense has been taught on this subject that we often fail to realize its real function. It goes back to the old Socratic "know thyself." When a man goes through college he ought to go through a general process of becoming acquainted with his own ability and desires so that by the time he graduates he will have a fairly clear idea of what place he can and ought to occupy in the world.

This means that the small college which I have in mind

would not be a professional school, would not be an industrial school, would not attempt to teach anybody how to earn a living. Its object would be to teach youth what the world is and what it means; and then after the college course we should learn the technique of earning a living in any way one can and wishes. The main job of such a college course is the unified cultural message. It takes the boy and shows him the world as it is with its customs and habits, its memories and ideals and works from that toward a vision of real life. Above all in our case it shows him our world—the one in which we live and must work.

For this reason the college should be closely integrated with its surrounding social setting. One of the great limitations of the older Negro college was that they came up with the idea of detachment from the town, city and state where they were. In part this was forced upon them by slavery and its consequences but it afterward became a habit; so that an intellectual class was trained which had no organic connection with the community around. In the small college which I have in mind this should no longer be true. The college should be an integral part of the community, of the colored community, of course, first; but also and just as needfully of the white community, so that in all its work and thinking, its government and art expression the community and college should be one and inseparable and at the same time the college could retain its leading function because of its independence and its clear ideals.

Such a college should be under the absolute control of the alumni: they should elect the trustees and hold them to strict account. Of course for such work the alumni themselves would need training: they would have to adopt a self-denying ordinance not to use their power to make jobs for themselves or children and to hold their power as a sacred trust for the education of a new and redeeming generation of men.

This may be a dream but it is worth considering.

Whither Now and Why

The American Negro has now reached a point in his progress where he needs to take serious account of where he is and whither he is going. This day has come much earlier than I thought it would. I wrote in 1940 a book called *Dusk of Dawn* in which I sought to record our situation in a period of change which I expected to last for another fifty years, but the Second World War and the rise of socialism and communism have hastened the event and we are definitely approaching now a time when the American Negro will become in law equal in citizenship to other Americans. There is much hard work yet to be done before the Negro becomes a voter, before he has equal rights to education and before he can claim complete civil and social equality. Yet this situation is in sight and it brings not as many assume an end to the so-called Negro problems, but a beginning of even more difficult problems of race and culture. Because what we must now ask ourselves is when we become equal American citizens what will be our aims and ideals and what will we have to do with selecting these aims and ideals. Are we to assume that we will simply adopt the ideals of Americans and become what they are or want to be and that we will have in this process no ideals of our own?

That would mean that we would cease to be Negroes as such and become white in action if not completely in color. We would take on the culture of white Americans doing as they do and thinking as they think.

Manifestly this would not be satisfactory. Physically it would mean that we would be integrated with Americans losing first of all, the physical evidence of color and hair and racial type. We would lose our memory of Negro history and of those racial peculiarities which have long been associated with the Negro. We would cease to acknowledge any greater tie with Africa than with England or Germany. We would not try to develop Negro music and Art and Literature as distinctive and different, but allow them to be further degraded as is the case today. We would always, if possible, marry lighter-hued people so as to have children who are not identified with the Negro race, and thus solve our racial problem in America by committing racial suicide. More or less clearly this possibility has been in the minds of Negroes in the past, although not assented to by all. Some have stated it and welcomed it. Others have simply assumed that this development was inevitable and therefore nothing could be done about it. This is the reason that my Pan-African Movement which began in 1900 when I cooperated with a meeting in London and definitely was started in 1919, in the first Pan-African Congress in Paris, could get but little support and cooperation among American Negroes. Most of them resented it as being a "back to Africa" movement. Others simply said we had problems enough in America without taking on the insoluble problems of Africa.

Today when the African people are arising to settle their own problems we are in peculiar position of being in a group of persons of Negro descent who not only cannot help the Africans but in most cases do not want to. Any statement of our desire to develop American Negro culture, to keep up our ties with coloured people, to remember our past is being regarded as "racism." I, for instance, who have devoted my life to efforts to break down racial barriers am being accused of desiring to emphasize differences of race. This has a certain truth about it. As I have said before and I repeat I am not fighting to settle the question of racial equality in America by the process of getting rid of the Negro race; getting rid of black folk, not producing black children, forgetting the slave trade and slavery, and the struggle for emancipation; of forgetting abolition and especially of ignoring the whole cultural history of Africans in the world.

No! What I have been fighting for and am still fighting for is the possibility of black folk and their cultural patterns existing in America without discrimination; and on terms of equality. If we take this attitude we have got to do so consciously and deliberately. This brings up a number of difficult problems which we will have to solve and make definite preparation for such solution.

Take for instance the current problem of the education of our children. By the law of the land today they should be admitted to the public schools. If and when they are admitted to these schools certain things will inevitably follow. Negro teachers will become rarer and in many cases will disappear. Negro children will be instructed in the public schools and taught under unpleasant if not discouraging circumstances. Even more largely than today they will fall out of school, cease to enter high school, and fewer and fewer will go to college. Theoretically Negro universities will disappear. Negro history will be taught less or not at all and as in so many cases in the past Negroes will remember their white or Indian ancestors and quite forget their Negro forebearers. Read for instance the autobiography of John Mercer Langston.

To some folk this type of argument would lead to the conclusion that we ought to refuse to enter white schools or to clamor for unsegregated schools. In other words that we ought to give up the fight against color discrimination. I want, however, to emphasize that this not only is unnecessary, but impossible. We must accept equality or die. What we must also do is to lay down a line of thought and action which will accomplish two things: The utter disappearance of color discrimination in American life and the preservation of African history and culture as a valuable contribution to modern civilization as it was to medieval and ancient civilization. To do this is not easy. It calls for intelligence, co-operation and careful planning. It would meet head on the baffling difficulties that face us today. Here for instance, is the boy who says simply he is not going to school. His treatment in the white schools even if he is admitted, is such that it does not attract him. Moreover, the boy who does enter the white school and gets on reasonably well does not always become a useful member of our group. Negro children educated in integrated schools and northern colleges often know nothing of Negro history. Know nothing of Negro leadership and doubt if there ever have been leaders in Africa, the West Indies and the United States who equal white folk. Some are ashamed of themselves and their folk. They regard the study of Negro biography and the writing of Negro literature as a vain attempt to pretend that Negroes are really the equal of whites. That tends to be the point of view of those of our children who are educated in white schools. There are going to be schools which do not discriminate against colored people and the number is going to increase slowly in the present, but rapidly in the future until long before the year 2000, there will be no school segregation on the basis of race. The deficiency in knowledge of Negro history and culture, however will remain and this danger must be met or else American Negroes will disappear. Their history and culture will be lost. Their connection with the rising African world will be impossible. What then can we do or should we try to do?

Negro parents and Negro Parent-Teacher Associations will have to at least temporarily, take on and carry the burden which they have hitherto left to the public schools. The child in the family, in specific organizations or in social life must learn what he will not learn in school until the public schools vastly improve. Negro history must be taught for many critical years by parents, in clubs by lecture courses, by a new Negro literature which Negroes must write and buy. This must be done systematically for the whole Negro race in the United States and elsewhere. This is going to take time and money and is going to call for racial organizations.

Negro communities, Negro private schools, Negro colleges will and must be organized and supported. This racial organization will be voluntary and not compulsory. It will not be discriminatory. It will be carried on according to definite object and ideal, and will be open to all who share this ideal. And of course that ideal must always be in accord with the greater ideals of mankind. But what American Negroes must remember is that voluntary organization for great ends is far different from compulsory segregation for evil purposes.

Especially and first there has got to be a deliberate effort made toward the building of Negro families. Our family organization has been left almost entirely to chance. How, when and where, the Negro boy and girl is going to meet and mate has been given no organized thought and in many cases the whole process has been deliberately ignored. Beyond that comes the primary question of what a Negro child is to do in life. This has been taught only incidentally and accidentally. The primary basis and end of life has not been guided by proper tuition in social sciences, in economics or in ethics, outside and beyond school; in the family and in religious organizations.

The Negro race has got to impress upon its children certain fundamental facts. The normal human being must work and work regularly to supply his wants, such legitimate wants as food, clothes and shelter. In addition there must be creative activities such as we understand under art and literature and then there must be systematic recreation for health, for normal satisfying of the sexual instinct, for social contact, for sympathy, friendship, love, and sacrifice.

In this matter of life vocation we Negroes have got to inculcate in the minds of our children many objects to which white America today is not only opposed but bitterly fights. Why should a man be a physician? Not simply to cure disease and treat accidents, but to prevent disease and protect health. Today most physicians have no time for this. This is the object of social medicine and is practiced in most of Europe, western and eastern, and in China. But in the United States, the American Medical Association fights with huge funds every effort to bring free government-supported social medicine to the service of the people. Why should a man study law but to see that justice is done; and yet the chief service and huge pay of lawyers today in America is to guide wealthy and powerful corporations in breaking the law and putting on the statute books laws which discriminate against the poor. Our jails are bursting with prisoners who have no one to defend them even when they have committed no crime. Why should a man become a dentist? Not to extract diseased teeth, but to prevent teeth from becoming diseased; by teaching dental therapy. The schools of the socialist and communist world are doing this. Our schools have scarcely begun. What is the object of business? Americans say, profits, and in order to make profits large we are spending $50 thousand million a year for war. This war is carried on to make exploitation of land and labor possible, to steal materials, and cheat laborers. When Northern Rhodesia sells her copper for $36 million she pays nothing for the land out of which this copper comes and only half a million for the black labor that mines it. Twenty million dollars goes to the investors and the rest to machines and white European labor. The true object of business should not be profit but service. The service of collecting raw material, processing it for consumption and bringing it to the consumer. For this service wages should be paid, but vast unearned income should not be given to the man who steals the land and takes from the laborer that which is his due. This is increasingly the belief of civilized countries, but it is not the belief of Western Europe nor of white America. The correct attitude toward vocations must then be taught increasingly in our schools. Yet today in American schools and colleges, white and black, economics, social science, money, and finance are not properly taught, and especially most schools and colleges are afraid to teach the remedies which socialism and communism propose for better distribution of work and income; or to tell how the larger part of the civilized world is adopting these methods of accomplishing these things. I pause to remark that your program committee has shown positive genius in not once mentioning the word "socialism" in this meeting. Yet socialism says most of the money which we pay for telephone service, for electrical devices and for power goes to make a few individuals rich and not for paying good wages or making these services cheap. Insurance is a great invention designed to place the cost of death and accident on the whole community instead of letting it ruin the individual. Here is no place for private profit. The premiums should pay for the loss and the wages of management should be included, but today above this individuals make millions, and private insurance companies control national money and credit. Evidently insurance is a public function and not a private enterprise.

The great American world of which we have for centuries been striving to become a part and which has arisen to be one of the most powerful nations is today losing its influence and that American Negroes do not realize. There was a time when as leader of a new democracy, as believers in a new tolerance in religion, and as a people basing their life on equality of opportunity, in the ownership of land and property, the United States of America stood first in the hopes of mankind. That day has passed. I took a trip recently that lasted nearly a year. I had already traveled widely. I had been to Europe fifteen times. I had been to Asia. I had circled the world. Then for nine years I was imprisoned in the confines of the United States by the unauthorized dictum of those who were ruling. From 1950 until 1958 I was not allowed to travel abroad. The reason was that I had cooperated with millions of men who wanted war to cease. Even here my action had been simply to tell Americans what was being done by other countries to promote peace. For this I was accused of being the agent of foreign peacemakers and ordered to admit this or go to jail. It cost me over $30,000 to defend myself in court against this absurd accusation. This sum I and my wife had to beg from state to state. The court threw the case out for lack of proof. Despite this I was refused a passport for travel abroad until the Supreme Court finally decided that the Department of State had no legal ground to refuse me a passport.

Paul Robeson, who for ten years had been deprived of a livelihood for equally baseless reasons, myself and others were given passports. I and my wife went abroad to Great Britain and Holland, to France and Czechoslovakia, to Sweden and Germany, to the Soviet Union and to the Chinese Republic. It was the most astonishing trip I have ever had. It radically changed my whole point of view. I saw first that America and its actions since the First World War was thoroughly condemned by the civilized world; that no other country was so disliked and hated. The British and the Dutch while restraining their expression of dislike behind good manners and for fear of our wealth and power, nevertheless, did not like America or Americans. That the French could hardly mention Americans without calling them dirty; that the people of Czechoslovakia and Germany blamed America for the cruelties which they suffered and for the difficulties which they were facing. That the 200 million people in the Soviet Union regard Americans as their greatest threat and the 680 millions of China hate America with perfect hatred for treating them as subhuman.

Outside this matter of feeling was my discovery that the world was going socialist, that most of the people of the world, Europe, Asia and Africa were either socialists or communists. No matter what our attitude toward socialism and communism may be, no matter how we judge the teachings of Karl Marx we must face the truth. Not only black but white Americans must know. We do not know.

The news gathering agencies and the periodicals of opinion in the United States are deliberately deceiving the people of the United States with regard to the rest of the world. For a long time they have spread the belief that communism is a crime or a conspiracy and that anyone either taking part or even examining conditions in socialist lands is a self-conscious criminal or a fool.

For decades now they have made Americans believe that communism is a failure, that the Russian people and the people of Hungary, Czechoslovakia and the Balkans were prisoners, enslaved in thought and action; that communism only needed our help to fall in ruin; that China is trying to conquer all Asia. Despite all this propaganda we are beginning now to realize some things that are clear. That the Soviet Union has made color prejudice illegal, that she has a system of education probably the best in the world and far superior to ours. That science there is forging ahead of anything that we have, and that the people are not prisoners and are not asking our help in order to revolt. They are progressing at a rate superior to us in art, literature and general happiness.

I spent thirteen weeks in China. I was treated with a courtesy I had met nowhere else in the world and I was convinced that here was a colored people who in happiness and knowledge would outstrip the world before the dawn of the next century. The work of China today is a miracle of success. What we Americans want is freedom to know the truth and the right to think and to act as seems wisest to us under the democratic process; and what we have to remember is that in the United States democracy has almost disappeared. There is no use deceiving ourselves in that respect. Half of the citizens of the United States do not even go to the polls. Most Negroes are disfranchised. It is the considered opinion of the social scientists in America that the election which made Dwight Eisenhower president cost over $100 million and perhaps $200 million. Why does America need such an election fund? A democratic election doesn't need it and the United States needed and used it only for bribing voters directly and indirectly or frightening men from acting or thinking. This is what the rulers of the United States demand and those rulers instead of being individuals are organized corporations who suppress freedom, by monopolizing wealth.

If all this true, it must be taught to our youth. It must be taught by teachers and instructors and professors and in that case we must face the fact that these teachers may lose their jobs. They can only be supported and employed if the bulk of American Negroes support institutions like the private Negro colleges. If the Negro or white colleges are going to depend on the gifts of the rich for support they cannot teach the truth. If they are supported tomorrow, Negroes must give not a tenth, but a quarter of their income to support education and social organization and teachers must sacrifice to the last penny. This impoverishment of the truth seekers can only be avoided by eventually making the state bear the burden of education and this is socialism. We must then vote for socialism. We began this in the New Deal and then were stopped. But in Europe and Asia and also in Africa socialism and communism are spreading. Socialism will grow in the United States if we restore the democracy of which we have boasted so long and done so little. Here is where Negroes may and must lead.

This is my sincere belief, arrived at after long study, travel, observation and thought. Many disagree with me and that is their right. They have every opportunity to express their belief and you cannot escape listening to them and should not if you could. But they have no right to demand that you refuse to listen to the world-wide voice of socialism or to threaten you with punishment if you do listen. This is the first right of democracy.

I appeal to the members of this organization, first to teach the truth as they see it even if they lose their jobs. To study socialism and communism and the philosophy of Karl Marx and his successors. To travel in the Soviet Union and China and then to dare take a stand as they honestly believe whether for or against communism. To refuse to listen to American propaganda without also listening to the propaganda of communism and to give up teaching and go to digging ditches before bowing to the new American slavery of thought. Above all to do everything possible to stop war and preparation for war which is the policy of the present rulers of this nation and their method of stopping socialism by force when they cannot stop it by work nor reason.

Bibliography

The Published Writings of W. E. B. Du Bois on Education

1) *Fisk* [University] *Herald,* October and November 1886 (on his teaching experiences in "The Hills of Tennessee").

2) *Fisk Herald,* Editorial, November 1887 (urges that Fisk seek independence from Northern philanthropists and that its finances come from Black people).

3) "Careers Open to College-Bred Negroes," in a pamphlet, *Two Addresses Delivered by Alumni of Fisk University, in Connection with the Anniversary Exercise of their Alma Mater* (Nashville: Fisk University Press [1898]) pp. 1–14. (The second address was by the Rev. H. H. Proctor.) Du Bois insists on the specific needs of Black colleges to serve Black people, calls for a more social Christianity, emphasizes the need for Black men and women in the professions, and closes by urging his listeners to "cherish unwavering faith in the blood of your fathers" and to serve without equivocation the causes of truth and freedom.

4) "A Negro Schoolmaster in the New South," *Atlantic Monthly,* January 1899; 83:99–104.

5) *A Memorial to the Legislature of Georgia on Negro Common Schools* (n.p., n.d.). This is a single-page, printed leaflet; it is signed by eight leading Black men of Georgia, including Du Bois, who wrote it. Though this is not indicated on the leaflet, it was printed in Atlanta in 1900.

6) *The College-Bred Negro,* edited by Du Bois (Atlanta, Ga.: Atlanta University Press, 1900), 115 pp.

7) *Memorial to the Legislature of Georgia on the Proposed Amendment Touching the Distribution of the School Fund* (n.p., n.d.) is a four-page leaflet, somewhat similar to no. 5 above. It bears fourteen signatures of leading Black men in Georgia; the list is headed by Du Bois, who wrote the *Memorial.* It was printed in Atlanta early in 1901.

8) Testimony given, February 13, 1901, in Washington before the Congressionally-appointed Industrial Commission, in Volume xv of the *Hearings on General and Industrial Education,* entitled Immigration and Education (Washington: Government Printing Office, 1901), pp. 159–75.

9) "The Burden of Negro Schooling," *Independent,* July 18, 1901; 53:1167–68.

10) *The Negro Common School . . .* (Atlanta, Ga.: Atlanta University Press, 1901), 119 pp.

11) "Of the Training of Black Men," *Atlantic Monthly,* September 1902; 90:289–97.

12) "Higher Education of the Negro," *Talladega College Record,* November 1902; 10:2.

13) "Of Mr. Booker T. Washington and Others," being Chapter iii of his *The Souls of Black Folk* (Chicago: A. C. McClurg, 1903); this was the only chapter of that classic written for the book. Much of it presents Du Bois's ideas, as of that date, on education. Nos. 4 and 11 above appeared as chapters in *Souls,* with some changes; the first under the title, "Of the Meaning of Progress" (Chapter iv) and the second under the above title (Chapter vi).

14) "The Training of Negroes for Social Power," the *Outlook,* October 17, 1903; 74:409–14. (This was reprinted in pamphlet form in 1903 by the Atlanta University Press; but the title was changed to read: *The Training of Negroes for Social Reform.*)

15) "The Talented Tenth," in *The Negro Problem* (a collection of essays by leading Black figures of the day; no editor is given. It was published in 1903 in New York City by James Pott Co.; Du Bois's very significant and influential essay appears on pp. 33–75).

16) *Heredity and the Public Schools: A Lecture Delivered under the Auspices of the Principals' Association of the Colored Schools of Washington, D.C., March 25, 1904* (Washington: R. L. Pendleton, 1904), 11 pp.

17) "The Joy of Living," a speech delivered in 1904 in Washington, probably at a high-school commencement, first published by the present editor, in *Political Affairs,* February 1965; 44: No. 2, 35–44; for details see introduction therein.

18) "What Intellectual Training Is Doing for the Negro," *The Missionary Review of the World,* August 1904; 17:578–82.

19) "Representative Higher Institutions for Negro Education in the South" (a lecture given in Boston, February 8, 1905), *Boston Globe,* February 9, 1905.

20) "Atlanta University," in *From Servitude to Service* (Boston: American Unitarian Association, 1905), pp. 155–97 (a collection of essays by various authors on Black institutions of education; no editor is given; at times, Du Bois has been proposed to have been the editor but this is certainly in error; probably the editor was Edwin D. Mead).

21) "The Hampton Idea," *Voice of the Negro,* September 1906; 3:332–36.

22) "St. Francis of Assisi," *Voice of the Negro,* October 1906; III, 419–26 (originally delivered before the Graduating Classes of the Colored High Schools of Washington, D.C., on June 15, 1906).

23) "Sociology and Industry in Southern Education," *Voice of the Negro,* May 1907; 4:170–75 (originally delivered at the University of Chicago on February 13, 1907).

24) "Negro Education and Evangelization," in *The New Schaff-Herzog Religious Encyclopedia,* edited by S. M. Jackson (New York: Funk & Wagnalls, 1910), 8:100–108.

25) *College-Bred Negro Communities: Address of Prof. W. E. B. Du Bois at Brookline, Mass.* (Atlanta, Ga.: 1910, Atlanta University Leaflet, No. 23), 16 pp.

*Asterisked essays appear in this volume.

26) *The College Bred Negro American* . . . , edited, with Augustus G. Dill (Atlanta, Ga.: Atlanta University Press, 1910), 104 pp.

27) *The Common School and the Negro American* . . . , edited, with Augustus G. Dill (Atlanta, Ga.: Atlanta University Press, 1911), 140 pp.

28) *Memorandum in Support of Proposed Amendment to H. R. 7951, Entitled a Bill to Provide for Co-operative Agricultural Extension Work Between the Agricultural Colleges in the Several States . . . and the U.S. Department of Agriculture.* (This sixteen-page pamphlet was issued by the NAACP in 1914. It is signed by Chapin Brinsmade as Attorney and by Du Bois as Director of Publicity and Research; it was written by Du Bois.)

Much of Du Bois's writings in the *Crisis,* which he edited from 1910 to the summer of 1934, dealt in one way or another with education, broadly defined, and many parts of his departments, such as "Postscript" and "As the Crow Flies," also touched this subject. Listed below (numbers 29–37), however, are those articles (signed and unsigned) by him in the *Crisis* which had as their subject in largest part, if not entirely, questions of education.

29) "Negro Education," February 1918; 15:173–78 (a long and critical [signed] evaluation of a book on the subject by Thomas Jesse Jones, who may be briefly characterized as the establishment's white "expert" on the subject).

30) "Colored Teachers in Charleston [S.C.] Schools," June 1921; 22:57–60 (signed).

31) "The Negro and the Northern Public Schools," two-part essay, March and April 1923; 25:205–8, 262–65 (unsigned).

32) "The Tragedy of Jim Crow," August, 1923; 26:169–72 (text of a speech delivered in Philadelphia before three thousand people—overwhelmingly Black—and dealing with the Cheyney State Normal School in Pennsylvania; this created heated debate for months thereafter).

33) "Fisk" (in his department, "Opinion"), October 1924; 28:251–52.

34) "Missouri Shows Us," September 1925; 30:226–27 (unsigned; deals with positive developments at Lincoln University in Missouri).

35) "Education in Africa," June 1926; 32:86–89 (a critical estimate, signed, of a two-volume report on the subject by, again, Thomas Jesse Jones; see above, number 29).

36) "Postscript," September 1929; 36:313–14, 317 (in this regular department, for this date, Du Bois deals with questions of segregated education).

37) "The Negro College," August 1933; 40:175–77, signed. (see below, number 43).

38) "To American Students," the *New Student*, December 1, 1923; 3:1.

39) "Diuturni Silenti," *Fisk Herald*, 1924; 33:i–xii.*

40) "Negroes in College," the *Nation*, March 3, 1926; 122:228–30.

41) "The Hampton [Institute Student] Strike," the *Nation*, November 2, 1927; 125:471–72.

42) "Education and Work," *Howard University Bulletin*, January 1931; 9:1–22;* and with some corrections in the *Journal of Negro Education*, April, 1932; 1:60–74 (a commencement address at Howard University, June 6, 1930).

43) *The Field and Function of a Negro College**
(Nashville: Fisk University Press, 1933), 16 pp.; a considerable excerpt was published in the *Crisis*, August 1933; 40:175–77 (delivered at the annual alumni reunion during Fisk's Commencement week, June, 1933).

44) "Does the Negro Need Separate Schools?" *Journal of Negro Education*, July 1935; 4:328–35.

45) Testimony, April 2, 1937, before Committee on Education, House of Representatives, 75th Cong., 1st Sess., *Hearings on Federal Aid for the Support of Public Schools* (Washington, D.C.: Government Printing Office, 1937), pp. 284–95.

46) "How Negroes Have Taken Advantage of Education Opportunities Offered by [the Society of] Friends," *Journal of Negro Education,* April 1938; 7:124–31.

47) "The Revelation of Saint Orgne the Damned," * *Fisk News,* November–December 1938; 9:3–9.

48) "The Future of Wilberforce University," *Journal of Negro Education,* October, 1940; 9:553–70.

49) "The Future of the Negro State University," * *Wilberforce University Quarterly,* April 1941; 2:53–60.

50) "A Program for the Land-Grant Colleges," in *Proceedings of the Nineteenth Annual Conference of the Presidents of Negro Land-Grant Colleges, November 11–13, 1941, Chicago* (n.p., n.d.), pp. 42–56.

51) "The Cultural Missions of Atlanta University," *Phylon,* 1942 (No. 2); 3:105–15.

52) *Report of the First Conference of Negro Land-Grant Colleges for Coordinating a Program of Cooperative Social Studies,* edited (Atlanta, Ga.: Atlanta University Press, 1943), 83 pp.

53) "Jacob and Esau," the *Talladegan,* November 1944; 42:1–6 address (delivered at Commencement, June 1944, at Talladega College in Alabama).

54) "The Future and Function of the Private Negro College," * the *Crisis,* August, 1946; 53:234–46, 253–54 (commencement address, Knoxville College, Tennessee, June, 1946).

55) "A Crisis at Fisk," the *Nation,* September 1, 1946; 163:269–70.

56) "No Second Class Citizenship," *Progressive Education,* January 1948; 25:10–14,21 (address delivered at the national convention of the American Education Fellowship, Chicago, November 1947).

57) "Two Hundred Years of Segregated Schools," *Jewish Life,* February 1955; 9: No. 4, 7–9, 15–18, 35.

58) "Whither Now and Why"* *Quarterly Review of Higher Education Among Negroes,* July 1960; 28:135–41 (delivered April 1960, at the 25th Annual Conference of the Association of Social Science Teachers, in Charlotte, N.C.).

For many years, in several newspapers, Du Bois contributed on a regular basis hundreds of columns. The subject of education frequently appears in parts of these but the list that follows indicates columns devoted wholly or in major part to one or another aspect of the question of education for Black people:

Amsterdam News

59) June 29, 1940: describes commencements he visited at Atlanta University, Wilberforce University and Harvard University; recalls briefly aspects of his Harvard days.

60) May 24, 1941: of his visits and lectures at Macalester College, the University of Minnesota and Northwestern University.

61) July 19, 1941: concerning Wilberforce University and problems of church and state rivalry.

62) March 7, 1942: heads of several New York colleges say they would welcome Black faculty members; they are lying and we should now flood them with applications and call their bluff.

63) April 25, 1942: devoted to an estimate of the history of Tuskegee.

64) May 16, 1942: has lectured at Vassar and Yale; this

induces observations about their élitism and racism, especially at Yale.

65) June 27, 1942: hails appointment of a Black professor (Allison Davis) at the University of Chicago; with continued effort, even Yale will one day become civilized.

66) July 4, 1942: an analysis of various aspects and phases of education.

67) September 5, 1942: a defense of college education if employed to acquire consequential knowledge.

68) May 29, 1943: we should battle more actively for the appointment of Black faculty members at so-called "white" universities.

Chicago Defender

69) October 6, 1945: segregated education is bad; and, above all, bad education is bad.

70) October 13, 1945: in opposing segregated education we must be careful not to demean Black teachers and youngsters.

71) May 18, 1946: "New Day at Lincoln University" in Pennsylvania because of the administration of Horace Mann Bond, its first Black president.

72) June 29, 1946: on summer schools: generally thinks them useless.

73) October 19, 1946: much boasting in the United States about education but on the whole it is quite poor.

74) April 12, 1947: has visited and comments upon state colleges for Black people in Durham, N.C., and Virginia State and Florida State.

75) June 7, 1947: details about the governance of Wilberforce and efforts to improve it (see above, no. 61).

76) November 29, 1947: an attack—evoked by an article in *Ebony* magazine—upon those who think "that the only goal for Negro intellectuals is to teach white people."

National Guardian

77) May 31, 1954: An analysis and estimate of the "School Segregation Decision" of the U.S. Supreme Court.

78) November 4, 1957: Returns to an examination of the 1954 decision, asking "What Is the Meaning of 'All Deliberate Speed' ? "

Finally, several of Du Bois's books treat one or another aspect of education. This has been noted above in connection with *The Souls of Black Folk.* In addition, *The Philadelphia Negro* (Philadelphia, 1899) deals at some length with the history, achievements and needs of education of Black people in that city; *Black Reconstruction in America* (New York, 1935) devotes dozens of pages to education, as one may find by consulting its index; his autobiographies—*Dusk of Dawn* (New York, 1940), and his posthumously published *A Soliloquy on Viewing my Life from the Last Decade of its First Century* (New York, 1968)—are filled with references to education, so that, for example, in the latter book Chapters 9,11,12, and 13 are devoted to this topic. Again, certain of his novels deal at length with education, this being an important theme in his *The Quest of the Silver Fleece* (Chicago, 1911) and in his trilogy, *The Black Flame,* especially its second volume, *Mansart Builds a School* (New York, 1959).

Index

Africa, 83, 115, 137, 144, 149, 151, 157. *See also individual countries*
Alabama, 97
Alpha Phi Alpha, 55
Amenia Conference, 61
American Labor party, 128
American Medical Association, 153
Amherst College, 142
Aristotle, 26, 107
Atlanta, Ga., 54, 62
Atlanta University, 18, 31, 32, 38, 40, 66, 102n., 142, 146

Babylonia, 26
Bantu people, 84
Bedales School, 41
Berlin, University of, 43, 89
Berne, Switzerland, 45
Birmingham, Ala., 50
birth-control, 106
Bontemps, Arna, 82n., 101
Boston, Mass., 39
Briand, Aristide, 77
British Empire, 77
Brookline, Mass., 31
Brooklyn (N.Y.) Girls' High School, 41
Brown, John, 115
Brown University, 44
Bruno, Giordano, 25
Bumstead, Horace, 31, 40

Cambridge University, 85
Chase, Frederick A., 57
Cheak, Rev. E. O., 13n.
Chesnutt, Charles W., 55, 56
Chicago, University of, 134
China, 153, 155, 156, 158
Church, Negro, 39, 113–14, 140

Church, Roman Catholic, 21–23
Cleveland, Ohio, 55–56
Columbia University, 134, 142
communism, 156, 158
Council on African Affairs, 127
Cravath, Erastus, 17, 56, 57
Crawford, George, 61
Crisis. 40, 82n., 97n., 101n.
culture: Afro-American, 149–50; nature of, 143–44
Czechoslovakia, 156

Dante Alighieri, 20
Davis, Harry, 55, 56
democracy, 52, 117–19, 156
disfranchisement, 91, 124
Dusk of Dawn, 149

Egypt, 26
Eliot, Charles W., 89
Elizabeth I, of England, 19
England, 19, 41, 85, 87, 149
equality, idea of, 118
ethics, problems of, 114
Eton, 85

family, the Negro, 152–53
Fisk Herald, 48, 60
Fisk News, 49, 50
Fisk University, 17, 19, 24, 27, 28, 30, 41, 42–59, 66, 81, 83, 88–89, 92, 99, 103, 141, 142, 143
Flexner, Abraham, 91
France, 93
fraternities, college, 51, 55, 67
freedom, its meaning, 116–17
French Revolution, 118

General Education Board, 17, 83
Georgia, 50, 110
Germany, 8n., 89–90, 149, 155

Gorky, Maxim, 20
Grant, Ulysses S., 20
Greece, 11n., 26, 47

Hamilton, Alexander, 20
Hampton Institute, 5, 6, 12, 13,
  16, 18, 57, 65, 66, 72, 81
Harlem Renaissance. *See*
  Renaissance, Harlem
Hart, Albert Bushnell, 89
Harvard University, 42, 56, 89,
  97, 130, 134, 141, 142
Haynes, George E., 18
Hopkins, Mark, 107
Howard University, 61, 66, 81,
  91, 94, 102
Hungary, 156
Hunton, W. Alphaeus, 127

Illinois, University of, 134
illiteracy, 34, 147
Indianapolis Freeman, 30
Indiana University, 134
Inquisition, 21
Italy, 20, 97

James, William, 89
Jews, 56, 120, 123
"Jim Crow," 50, 54, 56, 92, 121
Johnson, Mordecai, 61
Jones, Thomas E., 83

Kant, Immanuel, 107
Kenya, 87–88
Knoxville College (Tenn.), 127,
  142

labor movement, 72
Langston, John M., 151
League of Nations, 77
life, meaning of, 116
Lincoln, Abraham, 20
Lincoln University (Mo.), 127,
  135–36
Lincoln University (Pa.), 141

London, England, 150
Luther, Martin, 8n., 25

McKay, Claude, 100
McKenzie, Fayette A., 60
marriage, 106
Marx, Karl, 20, 102, 156, 157
Medici, Giovanni de', 21
Merrill, James G., 17, 30, 41
Michigan, University of, 143
Missouri, 129, 133–35
Missouri, University of, 135
Murray, Margaret (Mrs.
  Booker T. Washington), 17

Nashville, Tenn., 17, 18, 53, 62
National Association for the
  Advancement of Colored
  People, 40, 51
"New Deal", the, 102
New Orleans, 62
Nigeria, 137
North Carolina, University of,
  127

Ohio, 55, 129
Oxford University, 85

Pan-African Movement, 150
Paris, France, 150
passport, refused to Du Bois, 155
peace, 26, 128
Pennsylvania, University of, 134
Petrarch, Francesco, 20
Pisa, Italy, 19, 28
Poland, 97

Raleigh, N.C., 62
Reconstruction, era of, 33, 62,
  118, 131
Renaissance, Harlem, 95–96
Renaissance, Italian, 21
Reynal and Hitchcock,
  publishers, 127
Robeson, Paul, 127, 128, 155

Robespierre, Maximilien, 20
Roman Catholic Church. *See*
  Church, Roman Catholic
Rome, Italy, 11n., 26
Roosevelt, Theodore, 12
Royce, Josiah, 89
Russia *(USSR)*, 75, 102, 155,
  156, 158

Santayana, George, 89
Santillana, Giorgio de, 24n.
Scott, Isaiah, 56
sex, attitude toward, 106, 153
Shakespeare, William, 144
Shaler, Nathaniel, 89
Shaw University, 141
Slater Fund, 17
Smith, Johnson C., University,
  128
socialism, 90, 149, 153, 156, 157
Socrates, 12
soldiers, Black, 129
"Sorrow Songs," 97, 110
Souls of Black Folk, The, 5, 139
South America, 66, 144
Spain, 93
Spence, Arthur K., 57
Stark, L. C., 127
Streator, George S., 41, 60
strike: by students, 60; by
  workers, 97
Sudan, the, 84, 137
Sumner, Charles, 102

Sweden, 155

Talladega College, 142, 146
Tennessee Valley Authority
  (TVA), 125
Texas, 143
Treitschke, Heinrich von, 90
trial, of Du Bois, 155
Truman, Harry S, 127
Tuskegee Institute, 5, 18, 31, 57,
  61, 65, 66, 72, 81, 141

unions, trade, 73
Urban League, National, 18

Vanderbilt University, 92
Virginia Union University, 142

Washington, Booker T., 5, 17,
  30, 61, 64
Washington, Mrs. Booker T. *See*
  Murray, Margaret
wealth, distribution of, 74, 79,
  99, 110, 116, 122, 131, 154
West Indies, 66, 137, 144, 151
Wilberforce University, 136, 140
Williams College, 142
Wisconsin, University of, 143

Yale University, 61, 97, 134, 142
Yoruba people, 84
Young Men's Christian
  Association, 39